The Craziest Stories of World War 2

CRAFTED BY SKRIUWER

At **Skriuwer**, we're more than just a team—we're a global community of people who love books. In Frisian, "Skriuwer" means "writer," and that's at the heart of what we do: creating and sharing books with readers worldwide. Wherever you are in the world, **Skriuwer** is here to inspire learning.

Frisian is one of the oldest languages in Europe, closely related to English and Dutch, and is spoken by about **500,000 people** in the province of **Friesland** (Fryslân), located in the northern Netherlands. It's the second official language of the Netherlands, but like many minority languages, Frisian faces the challenge of survival in a modern, globalized world.

We're using the money we earn to promote the Frisian language.

For more information, contact : **kontakt@skriuwer.com** (www.skriuwer.com)

Disclaimer:
The images in this book are creative reinterpretations of historical scenes. While every effort was made to accurately capture the essence of the periods depicted, some illustrations may include artistic embellishments or approximations. They are intended to evoke the atmosphere and spirit of the times rather than serve as precise historical records.

TABLE OF CONTENTS

CHAPTER 1: A WORLD ON EDGE

- *Global tensions grow after World War I*
- *Extremist politics and territorial ambitions*
- *Japan's push into Manchuria and China*

CHAPTER 2: EARLY SURPRISES AND ODD EVENTS

- *Lightning war tactics in Poland*
- *Unexpected invasions of Denmark and Norway*
- *The Dunkirk evacuation miracle*

CHAPTER 3: STRANGE TECHNOLOGIES AND SECRET PLANS

- *Enigma codebreaking and Allied countermeasures*
- *First jet engines and rocket programs*
- *Inflatable tanks and ghost armies*

CHAPTER 4: UNBELIEVABLE MISSIONS BEHIND ENEMY LINES

- *Norwegian heavy water sabotage*
- *SAS raids in the North African desert*
- *Skorzeny's daring rescue of Mussolini*

CHAPTER 5: ANIMALS IN SERVICE AND BIZARRE STRATEGIES

- *War horses, carrier pigeons, and bat bombs*
- *Operation Fantasia and other strange plans*
- *Animal mascots raising troop morale*

CHAPTER 6: MISCOMMUNICATIONS AND LUCKY ESCAPES

- *Dunkirk's pause order and mass evacuation*
- *Radio mix-ups and friendly fire incidents*
- *Operation Market Garden's tragic confusion*

CHAPTER 7: THE GHOST ARMIES AND DECEPTION TACTICS

- *Operation Fortitude's inflatable tanks*
- *Soviet maskirovka and camouflage methods*
- *Audio illusions and fake landing craft*

CHAPTER 8: SPIES, LIES, AND CODEBREAKERS

- *British SOE, American OSS, and Soviet NKVD*
- *Double agents like Garbo misleading Germany*
- *Enigma and Purple cipher breakthroughs*

CHAPTER 9: UNEXPECTED ALLIANCES AND STRANGE FRIENDSHIPS

- *The Soviet-German Non-Aggression Pact*
- *Italy's shift from Axis to Allied partner*
- *Neutral nations with hidden involvements*

CHAPTER 10: WEAPONS THAT SHOCKED THE WORLD

- *Tank innovations and massive battleships*
- *V-1 buzz bombs and V-2 rockets*
- *The atomic bomb's earth-shattering debut*

CHAPTER 11: THE WILDEST CHARACTERS OF THE WAR

- *Churchill, Hitler, and Stalin's unique traits*
- *Famous generals like Patton and Rommel*
- *Everyday heroes such as Audie Murphy*

CHAPTER 12: DARING NAVAL ADVENTURES AND SUBMARINE TALES

- *The Atlantic U-boat struggle and convoy defense*
- *Hunting the Bismarck and carrier warfare*
- *Kamikaze strikes and naval last stands*

CHAPTER 13: MIRACULOUS SURVIVAL STORIES

- *Trapped under rubble during bombings*
- *Adrift on rafts after ship sinkings*
- *Survival in jungles, deserts, and front lines*

CHAPTER 14: PECULIAR PRISONER ESCAPES AND CAMP TALES

- *Stalag Luft III's "Great Escape"*
- *Colditz Castle's glider plan*
- *Civilians in internment and forced-labor camps*

CHAPTER 15: THE HOME FRONT – ODD HAPPENINGS AWAY FROM BATTLE

- *Rationing, black markets, and creative cooking*
- *Child evacuations and nightly blackouts*
- *Shifting social roles and urban rumors*

CHAPTER 16: THE POWER OF PROPAGANDA AND WEIRD INFLUENCES

- *Goebbels, Stalin, and Allied propaganda efforts*
- *Leaflet drops, radio shows, and bizarre claims*
- *Hollywood films fueling war morale*

CHAPTER 17: MEDICAL MARVELS AND CURIOUS HOSPITAL STORIES

- *Field surgeries, blood transfusions, and penicillin*
- *Caring for civilians in bombed-out cities*
- *Secret rescues and innovative treatments*

CHAPTER 18: HIDDEN TREASURES AND STRANGE FINDS

- *Nazi looting of European art collections*
- *Mysterious gold trains and Yamashita's treasure*
- *Buried family valuables and stashed archives*

CHAPTER 19: NEAR THE END – STRANGE TWISTS AS THE WAR CLOSED

- *The Ardennes surprise and the Battle of the Bulge*
- *Hitler's final days and conspiracy rumors*
- *Japan's kamikaze missions and atomic bombings*

CHAPTER 20: AFTERMATH AND UNRESOLVED MYSTERIES

- *Rebuilding ruined cities and war crimes trials*
- *Cold War seeds and displaced populations*
- *Lingering searches for missing people and loot*

CHAPTER 1

A World on Edge

World War II did not begin suddenly. It was the result of many events and tensions that built up during the 1930s. After World War I ended in 1918, countries in Europe tried to recover from the large-scale destruction. However, Germany faced heavy punishments under the Treaty of Versailles. This treaty demanded Germany pay huge sums of money and follow strict rules. Many Germans felt angry and humiliated, which created a fertile ground for extremist ideas to grow.

At the same time, other countries were also in difficult positions. The Great Depression of the 1930s affected nations all around the world. Jobs were lost, families struggled to find food, and governments often failed to help in time. These conditions opened doors for strong leaders who promised to restore wealth and power. In Italy, Benito Mussolini rose to power, preaching a new form of government called Fascism. In Germany, Adolf Hitler led the National Socialist German Workers' Party, also known as the Nazi Party. He promised to rebuild the economy, create jobs, and restore German pride.

The tension was not only in Europe. In Asia, Japan had a growing empire. It looked for more resources to support its industry and army. Japan invaded Manchuria in 1931 and later went deeper into China, causing conflicts that foreshadowed an even larger war. Meanwhile, the Soviet Union, under Joseph Stalin, was also growing stronger. Though its people suffered under harsh government policies, the Soviet Union had a vast territory and a powerful army.

All these elements caused fear and uncertainty across the globe. By the late 1930s, war seemed almost certain, even though many people still hoped to avoid a conflict as terrible as World War I. But new leaders were not interested in peace. They had plans to expand their territories, gain resources, and increase their influence. While some countries tried to negotiate peace, others secretly planned invasions and formed alliances.

The Rise of Adolf Hitler

Adolf Hitler became Chancellor of Germany in 1933. He was a strong speaker who used Germany's economic hardships and anger from World War I to rally support. Once in power, he began to ignore the Treaty of Versailles by building up the German military. He also made alliances with Italy and later with Japan. Hitler wanted to unite all German-speaking people in one large empire. He also blamed Jewish people and others for Germany's problems, promoting hateful ideas that would lead to horrifying events.

Many European leaders did not want to start another war. They remembered the horrors of World War I and chose a policy called appeasement. This meant giving in to some of Hitler's demands in hopes that he would be satisfied and stop. But Hitler did not stop. He took more and more risks, and soon, large parts of Europe faced the threat of Nazi expansion.

Mussolini and Italian Ambitions

Benito Mussolini took power in Italy in the early 1920s. He wanted to revive the glory of the old Roman Empire. Under Fascism, he aimed to create a strong Italy that dominated the Mediterranean region. Mussolini invaded Ethiopia (then called Abyssinia) in 1935. The League of Nations, an international organization set up after World War I to keep peace, tried to resist him with economic sanctions. But they were not strong enough. Mussolini's successful invasion inspired other leaders who saw that the League of Nations was weak.

Japan's Expansion in Asia

Japan's empire was growing rapidly. It needed raw materials like coal, oil, and iron. The government decided that controlling nearby regions would give them the resources they needed. This led Japan to invade Manchuria in 1931 and launch a full-scale war on China in 1937. Japanese armies used brutal tactics, causing fear and suffering. Western powers like the United States and Britain worried, but they were not yet ready for a fight in Asia.

Alliances and Secret Pacts

While mistrust spread across the world, leaders made secret deals to protect their own interests. Germany and the Soviet Union signed the Non-Aggression Pact in August 1939. This meant that if Germany invaded Poland, the Soviet Union would not intervene. In return, Stalin would get parts of Poland and the Baltic states. This surprised many people because communism and Nazism seemed like total opposites. But in politics, convenience often comes before principles.

Germany also grew closer to Italy, and both grew closer to Japan. The three countries would later form the Axis Powers. Their enemies became the Allied Powers, led mainly by Britain, the Soviet Union (after Germany betrayed them later), and the United States (which joined after Japan's attack on Pearl Harbor in 1941). But early on, things were not so clear, and people hoped war could still be avoided.

The Spark That Lit the Fire

The final spark that lit the fuse of World War II was Germany's invasion of Poland on September 1, 1939. Britain and France had promised to protect Poland, so they declared war on Germany.

However, they could not help Poland right away. Germany's blitzkrieg (lightning war) tactics overwhelmed Polish defenses. Soon, the Soviet Union also invaded Poland from the east, following the secret terms of the Non-Aggression Pact.

The fall of Poland marked the first major operation of World War II in Europe. Over the next few months, countries across Europe started preparing for an all-out war. Many thought it would mirror the trench warfare of World War I. But technology had advanced, and strategies had changed. Airplanes, tanks, and motorized vehicles were more important than ever before, and battles took place quickly across large areas.

Strange Atmosphere at the Start

During the early months of the war, there was an odd calm period in Western Europe called the "Phony War" or "Sitzkrieg." Britain and France had declared war, but there were no major actions on the Western Front right away. Soldiers from the Allied countries sat waiting along the borders, expecting a German attack. The war felt both close and far away at the same time. Families back home worried but still tried to live normal lives.

During these months, Hitler was busy securing his hold on Poland and planning further invasions. In April 1940, Germany suddenly moved against Denmark and Norway. This bold move forced the Allies to realize that Germany was not planning to stay still. Within weeks, the "Phony War" ended, and the real fighting began in full force.

Beginning of Strange and Crazy Stories

Even at this early stage, odd things happened that hinted at how strange this war would be. There were stories of daring spy missions, unusual alliances, and surprising acts of kindness. For instance, in some places, German and Allied soldiers had small truces for a few hours to gather their wounded. This kind of courtesy did not last long, but it showed that even in a large conflict, individuals could act in unexpected ways.

As the war grew, leaders and armies tried new tactics. Some of these methods sounded almost comical. For example, attempts were made to train animals for special missions. Spies carried messages in hollow coins or disguised themselves in silly ways to fool guards. Scientists worked on experimental bombs and weapons that never saw widespread use but were bizarre in theory. From the creation of inflatable tanks to weird radio signals meant to trick enemy troops, World War II quickly turned into a stage for many wild inventions and events.

In the chapters that follow, we will explore these stories in detail. From the early days of the war to its final hours, strange and surprising moments popped up in every theater of conflict—land, sea, and air. We start with how the war spread rapidly, grabbing the attention of the whole world.

The Human Side of Fear

When Germany invaded Poland, the Polish people faced immediate terror. They found themselves bombed by the Luftwaffe (the German air force) and attacked by fast-moving tanks. Civilians tried to flee cities, crowding onto roads that were also used by the military. Fear spread across Europe as everyone realized that the war had truly begun. Families in Britain and France also braced themselves. Many children were sent to the countryside to stay safe from bombings. The atmosphere was tense and strange. People heard about modern war machines—like dive bombers and huge tanks—and worried that cities would be destroyed in minutes.

For many, life became a mixture of normal routine and sudden panic. Some nights were filled with air-raid sirens. Other days, they tried to keep businesses and schools open. Soldiers were trained, sent to bases, and given orders to stand by. This sense of waiting for something terrible to happen made for a very uneasy mood.

Social Changes and Odd Reactions

Societies in the war-torn countries had to adjust quickly. Men went to fight, women took on work in factories, and people in rural areas had to feed growing armies. Rationing of food, clothes, and gasoline became normal. This often led to unusual ways of cooking meals or reusing old items. People tried to be creative with whatever they had. Children learned to recognize different plane engine sounds so they could identify enemy bombers.

Despite the seriousness of it all, moments of humor and odd occurrences brightened the gloom. For example, in Britain, people painted white stripes on trees and lampposts so they wouldn't bump into them during blackouts. Sometimes soldiers were given leaflets describing how to stay calm while wearing a gas mask. These leaflets could sound both silly and scary at the same time.

Early Heroes and Villains

War always produces both heroes and villains. At the start, many leaders made decisions that would define them in history. Winston Churchill became Prime Minister of Britain in May 1940, and his strong speeches would inspire many. On the villain side, leaders like Hitler made choices that led to untold suffering. Civilians in occupied countries had to learn how to survive under harsh conditions. Some formed resistance groups, while others tried to hide or escape.

At times, these resistance groups carried out brave missions to disrupt enemy plans. They might blow up a bridge or send secret messages to Allied forces. This was especially risky because getting caught often led to terrible punishments. Yet, many people decided that risking their own safety was worth it, hoping to help free their country from occupation.

Looking Toward the Future

By the end of 1939, it was clear that this war would involve much of the world. Colonies in Africa and Asia were connected to European powers, and so their people also got pulled into the conflict. The United States tried to stay neutral, but it provided weapons to Britain and other Allies through programs like "Lend-Lease." As for the Soviet Union, it sat in a tense relationship with Germany—on paper, they were allies, but many knew it would not last.

In the next chapter, we will explore the early surprises and odd events that took place when fighting erupted in full force. We will see how some invasions happened in ways nobody expected and how luck or misfortune changed the course of battles. And we will start hearing about the wild stories that set World War II apart, from a soldier who captured a dozen enemies single-handedly to bizarre accidents that changed the outcome of entire campaigns.

This first chapter lays the groundwork for all that will follow. It is important to understand how the world got to this point and why so many nations were ready—or forced—to take part in a conflict of such scale. With the stage set, we can dive into the strange stories and events that made World War II one of the most unbelievable and wide-ranging conflicts in human history.

CHAPTER 2

Early Surprises and Odd Events

When the war began in earnest after Germany invaded Poland, it quickly spread in unexpected ways. While most people expected heavy fighting on the eastern and western fronts in Europe, no one foresaw the strange turns events would take. Unexpected invasions, wild weather changes, and unusual acts of bravery and foolishness colored these first stages of conflict. In this chapter, we will explore some early surprises and odd events that set the tone for a war filled with twists and turns.

The Blitzkrieg Shock

Germany's attack on Poland introduced the world to "blitzkrieg," a lightning-fast style of warfare. In earlier wars, armies lined up and fought on battlefields for days or even weeks in slow-moving engagements. Now, fast-moving tanks, mechanized troops, and air power combined to strike the enemy with speed. This tactic relied on surprise, communication by radio, and concentrated force. Poland's older style of defense could not hold back the German forces.

But along with the success of blitzkrieg came odd failures. On multiple occasions, German tanks ran out of fuel because the speed of their advance was so rapid. In some cases, they had to wait for supply trucks to catch up. Yet even these delays did not save Poland. In a matter of weeks, Poland was split between Germany and the Soviet Union, as agreed in their secret pact.

Strange Battle Outcomes

While the outcome in Poland was grim, other parts of Europe saw curious results. Germany invaded Denmark and Norway in April 1940. Denmark surrendered almost immediately, hoping to spare its people from destruction. However, Norway resisted. German troops landed at several Norwegian ports, and the Norwegian army fought back with the help of British and French forces. This led to battles in the cold Norwegian winter mountains, where many soldiers were not prepared for freezing conditions.

There are stories of entire squads getting lost in blizzards and stumbling upon enemy positions by accident. The darkness and snow led to mistaken shootings between allies. In some moments, small local groups of Norwegian volunteers fought with skis, surprising the Germans who were not used to that kind of movement in the snow. In one case, a group of Norwegian skiers managed to capture a German position by attacking from behind in near-silence. These unusual winter tactics shocked Germany, which was more accustomed to rapid tank advances on regular roads. Still, Norway eventually fell under German control, but not without making the invasion longer and more costly than Hitler had hoped.

The Ardennes Surprise

Hitler's next move surprised everyone. Instead of charging across the heavily defended borders of France, the German army went through the Ardennes Forest, a region in Belgium that was considered too tough for tanks to pass. French and British commanders believed the dense forest and narrow roads would prevent a major tank invasion. To their shock, German divisions, using special engineering units, cleared paths through the woods. Their tanks emerged where the Allies did not expect them, outflanking the Maginot Line (France's main line of defense).

This led to the swift fall of France in June 1940. The Allies were pushed back to the French beaches at Dunkirk. There, in one of the war's early miracles, more than 300,000 Allied soldiers were evacuated across the English Channel by a mix of naval vessels and civilian boats. This rescue, known as the Dunkirk evacuation, was a strange and heroic event. British fishing trawlers, merchant ships, and even private yachts crossed dangerous waters under air attack to pick up stranded soldiers. The German forces hesitated for a couple of days near Dunkirk, giving the Allies the time they needed to organize the escape. Historians still debate why Hitler halted his tanks, but that pause helped save a large part of the British Army.

The Curious Tale of the "Sitzkrieg"

Before these invasions, from late 1939 to early 1940, the war in Western Europe seemed oddly quiet. This period was nicknamed the "Phony War" or "Sitzkrieg." German and Allied forces faced each other along the French-German border, but neither side launched a major attack. Soldiers spent their days training, shoveling snow, and waiting. Some folks back home started to doubt if a real war would happen after all.

However, the calm hid plenty of strange small incidents. For example, on one occasion, a German pilot got lost in fog and landed by mistake on a Belgian airfield. He carried secret attack plans for Belgium in his plane. When Belgian officers discovered this, it proved that Germany was planning to move through Belgium to reach France. This forced the Allies to prepare, though it did not stop Germany's eventual success. The pilot's embarrassing mistake became a news story at the time, though it did little to change the outcome.

Odd Encounters at Sea

Away from land battles, the war at sea also had its share of strange moments. Germany had a fleet of U-boats (submarines) that hunted

Allied ships carrying supplies. Early in the war, a U-boat sank a passenger liner called the SS Athenia on the very first day of the war, causing shock. But not all encounters were tragic. Sometimes, U-boat crews surfaced to let passengers on smaller ships climb into lifeboats, showing an odd sense of chivalry before sinking the vessel. This practice faded as the war intensified.

One of the strangest naval tales was the fate of the German pocket battleship Admiral Graf Spee. It raided Allied merchant ships in the South Atlantic and Indian Ocean, but treated captured crews fairly. The British hunted for it with several warships. Eventually, the Graf Spee took refuge in Uruguay's Montevideo harbor. Thinking British reinforcements were on the way, the captain scuttled (deliberately sank) his own ship to prevent capture, then took his own life. In fact, the British force was not as strong as he believed. This piece of misinformation and the captain's hasty choice made the Graf Spee story famous as an early war oddity.

Italy Joins In

While Germany was conquering Europe at lightning speed, Italy was slow to act. Mussolini declared war on France and Britain in June 1940, just when France was on the brink of collapse. Italy hoped to grab territory and share in Germany's victory without fighting too hard. But Italy's armies were not ready for modern war. Their attacks often ended in confusion or quick retreats, such as in Greece and North Africa, creating surprising results. In fact, the Greek Army pushed back Italian forces, and this failure led Hitler to intervene in the Balkans. These entangled operations would open up even more fronts in the war, each with its own odd events and surprises.

Crazy Weather Interference

The weather played a crucial role in many of the early battles. In Norway, snow and frost caused tanks to get stuck. In France, unexpected storms kept planes grounded. Poor weather sometimes saved one side from a major attack. For example, Germany once postponed a large operation because of thick fog, only to discover that postponement allowed them to spot a hidden Allied trap. Weather events worked both for and against all sides, adding to the strange unpredictability of the war.

Some accounts describe how entire columns of vehicles were lost in sudden snowstorms. In the Soviet Union, where the war would later expand, the harsh winter became legendary. But even in the early stages, unpredictable weather helped shape outcomes. Soldiers from warmer climates struggled in freezing conditions, while northern troops found it hard to cope with hot deserts. These mismatches led to unexpected captures, rescues, and sometimes the end of entire campaigns.

Bizarre Instances of Neutral Countries

Several European countries remained neutral or tried to stay out of the conflict. Switzerland and Sweden, for instance, did not join the war. However, even these nations got dragged into strange skirmishes. Allied and Axis planes sometimes flew over their airspace, and some crashed or made emergency landings. When that happened, the neutral country had to decide whether to hold the crews or let them go. Rules about neutrality were tested in odd ways.

In Sweden, a number of British and American crews who crash-landed were interned, but were sometimes treated well and even allowed to find work. This led to unusual friendships between local people and foreign airmen. Meanwhile, Spain, under dictator Francisco Franco, officially stayed neutral but leaned toward the Axis. Many Germans traveled through Spain to fight in North Africa or to spy on Allied forces. These side activities often looked more like cloak-and-dagger stories than typical warfare.

Early Resistance Movements

Although Germany occupied several countries in quick succession, resistance groups sprang up almost immediately. In Poland, France, Norway, and other places, small bands of fighters refused to accept Nazi control. They passed on valuable intelligence, rescued Allied soldiers, and performed acts of sabotage like destroying train tracks or communication lines. Some groups had creative ways of hiding messages, such as stuffing notes into hollow book bindings or carving secret codes into bread loaves.

One odd event involved a Polish spy who dressed up as a mailman and casually walked into a German command post, stealing documents right off a desk. He then strolled out, with guards barely giving him a second look. Later, his group used those documents to plan a sabotage operation that disrupted German communications for days. Acts like this showed that, even though the Axis had overwhelming power, brave individuals found clever ways to fight back.

Clash of Old and New Tactics

The early war period saw old-fashioned tactics collide with modern technology. Cavalry units on horseback still existed, especially in Poland, facing off against German tanks. Pilots fought dogfights in the sky like World War I aces, but now they had improved airplanes with heavier bombs and better engines. Battleships still roamed the seas, but they were vulnerable to air power and submarines. These mismatches produced some odd moments, like cavalry charges against armored vehicles, which usually ended in tragedy.

At the same time, countries tested new weapons that sounded more like science fiction. Germany launched the development of rockets and early guided missiles. Britain explored radar technology to detect incoming enemy planes. Some scientists proposed ideas like bat bombs or tiny submarines for sabotage. Although not all these concepts saw real use, the creativity was astounding.

Diplomatic Oddities

There were also strange events in diplomacy. Germany and the Soviet Union pretended to be friends, but no one believed this would last. Countries like Hungary, Romania, and Bulgaria were bullied into joining the Axis or risked invasion. Meanwhile, smaller nations like Belgium and the Netherlands tried to remain neutral as long as possible, only to be invaded by Germany when it suited Hitler's plans.

In one strange case, German diplomats in a neutral country found themselves stuck when war broke out. With travel restricted, they used fake names and disguised themselves to sneak back to Germany through different borders. Allied agents sometimes intercepted these diplomats and traded them for their own captured officials. Such cloak-and-dagger stories were a minor but fascinating part of the larger war machine.

The Unexpected Collapse of France

Perhaps the biggest surprise of the early war was how quickly France fell. After World War I, France had invested heavily in the Maginot Line, a series of fortresses along the German border. But the Germans bypassed it by going through the Low Countries and the Ardennes Forest. In just six weeks, France was forced to sign an armistice. This stunned the world. Everyone believed World War I had proven France's military strength, yet now it had crumbled under the blitzkrieg.

The division of France into the occupied north and the Vichy government in the south led to many odd situations. Some French officials cooperated with Germany, while others fled to Britain, where Charles de Gaulle encouraged the French to continue fighting. Resistance networks formed inside France, creating a hidden war of secret messages and sabotage. This set the stage for countless stories of bravery, betrayal, and even bizarre comedic moments, like the forging of documents using stolen German typewriters.

Britain Stands Alone

By mid-1940, Britain stood alone against the might of Germany in Western Europe. People expected an invasion of Britain at any moment. Hitler planned "Operation Sea Lion," a large-scale invasion across the English Channel. But before he could launch it, he needed air superiority. This led to the Battle of Britain, a fierce air campaign between the German Luftwaffe and the British Royal Air Force (RAF).

In a strange twist, Britain's use of radar allowed them to detect incoming German planes. Spitfires and Hurricanes scrambled to meet the raiders. Every day, the British listened for the wail of air-raid sirens. Many took shelter in underground stations in London. Oddly enough, some families tried to continue daily life underground, bringing blankets and small cooking stoves. Children would do homework by candlelight as bombs fell above. Despite heavy losses, the RAF managed to hold off the Luftwaffe, causing Hitler to postpone his invasion plans. This was another early turning point, and it gave hope to occupied nations.

Crazy Ideas to Protect Britain

During this time, Britain also came up with strange ideas to defend itself. One plan was to create "sticky bombs" that would attach to enemy tanks. Another involved training special units to hide in the countryside and attack German forces from behind if they landed. Even everyday objects could become booby traps. There was talk of placing explosives in farm fields or even covering beaches with barbed wire and sharpened stakes to stop enemy landings.

People in small towns practiced how to fight an invader. They stored simple weapons like shotguns, pitchforks, and knives. Some practiced climbing walls or digging hidden tunnels. While many of these plans were never tested in real combat, they show how desperate times led people to think outside the box.

The War Grows Wider

Even as these events unfolded, the war spread beyond Europe. Italy had colonies in Africa and clashed with British forces in places like Egypt and Sudan. Japan continued its war in China and eyed the European colonies in Southeast Asia. The United States remained neutral but began helping Britain by sending war supplies. Across the world, everyone watched and waited to see if the war would end quickly or grow into something even bigger. As we now know, it grew and grew until it engulfed nearly every continent.

Stories That Captured the Public's Attention

Despite the grim realities, newspapers and radio broadcasts were filled with stories that sometimes sounded like movie plots. For example, a British pilot shot down three enemy bombers in a single flight and then bailed out of his damaged plane, only to parachute onto the roof of a barn and land unharmed. Another story told of a French civilian who biked through enemy lines at night to deliver crucial information to a British commander. When asked how he avoided capture, he replied that the Germans did not believe anyone would dare bike alone in the dark.

People clung to these tales of bravery and luck, finding hope in them. They also shared stories of small mistakes that turned into big problems for the enemy. If a radio operator forgot the correct code, confusion could lead an entire unit to the wrong location. In a war so large, even tiny errors could have huge impacts.

Preparing for the Next Phase

By the end of 1940, much of Europe lay under German control, Britain stood defiant, and the Soviet Union watched carefully from the east. Italy struggled in its campaigns, and Japan planned more moves in Asia. The United States was not yet at war, but many suspected it was only a matter of time. People around the world braced themselves for an even larger conflict. Little did they know how wild and desperate the war would become in the years ahead.

In the next chapter, we will explore the strange technologies and secret plans that both Allied and Axis powers developed. From codebreaking machines like the German Enigma to the Allied invention of new bombs, the war became a race of innovation as each side tried to gain the upper hand. We will see how some projects were so bizarre that they never got beyond the planning stage, while others changed the course of the war.

CHAPTER 3

Strange Technologies and Secret Plans

World War II was not just a war of tanks and airplanes. It was also a war of ideas, inventions, and secret projects. Both the Axis powers (Germany, Italy, and Japan) and the Allied powers (Britain, the Soviet Union, the United States, and others) worked day and night to find new ways to surprise or overpower their enemies. Many of these ideas were serious and would shape modern warfare. Others were strange and even a bit laughable. But at the time, nations were desperate to gain any advantage they could, so they were willing to try almost anything.

The Race for Better Weapons

From the very start of the war, governments realized that older weapons might not be enough. After seeing how effective German tanks and dive-bombers (like the Stuka) were during the invasion of Poland and France, the Allies understood they needed stronger defenses. Factories in Britain, the Soviet Union, and the United States began producing new models of tanks, airplanes, and ships at a rapid pace.

In Germany, Adolf Hitler pushed his scientists and engineers to develop "wonder weapons" (in German, called *Wunderwaffe*). He believed these special new weapons could turn the tide of battle in Germany's favor, especially after things got tougher on the Eastern Front against the Soviet Union and in the skies over Britain. Many of these projects required large budgets, secret labs, and teams of experts. While some of these weapons did appear in battle, others never left the drawing board.

The Enigma Machine and Codebreaking

One of the most famous pieces of World War II technology was the Enigma machine. It looked like a typewriter with wheels, but it allowed German forces to send coded messages that they believed could not be broken. Each day, the wheels (or rotors) in the Enigma machine would be set to a new arrangement, creating millions of possible ways to scramble the letters. German commanders used Enigma machines on land, in the air, and especially in their U-boats at sea.

However, Allied codebreakers (most famously working at Bletchley Park in Britain) managed to figure out how to read many Enigma messages. They built early computers, called "bombes," and other devices to break the Enigma code. This gave the Allies secret knowledge of German plans, which helped them win key battles in the Atlantic and elsewhere. Because the work was top secret, very few people knew about it during the war. Soldiers on the front lines had no idea that some of their orders were guided by information from broken German codes. This codebreaking success was one of the greatest secrets of the war.

Japan's Codes and the Purple Machine

Germany was not the only Axis power that used advanced code systems. Japan also had complex cipher machines, including one nicknamed "Purple" by the Americans. By carefully studying intercepted messages, Allied codebreakers eventually worked out how to read a good number of Japan's coded communications. This helped the United States plan naval battles in the Pacific. For example, the breaking of Japanese codes played a major role in the American victory at the Battle of Midway in 1942. Because of that victory, Japan's naval power in the Pacific began to weaken.

Radar: Seeing Planes in the Sky

Before World War II, radar was a brand-new idea. Radar stands for "radio detection and ranging." It works by sending out radio waves that bounce off objects, like airplanes. By measuring how long it takes for the waves to come back, a radar station can tell where and how far away the object is. Britain used radar stations along its coastline to watch for incoming German bombers during the Battle of Britain. This gave British pilots extra time to scramble and get into the air to meet the enemy. Radar helped make up for the fact that Germany had more planes. Thanks to radar, the British could organize their fighters more efficiently, saving precious fuel and aircraft. Germany did not realize at first how advanced British radar technology was, so this proved to be a big advantage for Britain.

The Early Jets

During the war, both Germany and Britain worked on jet airplane engines. German scientists led the way with planes like the Messerschmitt Me 262, the first operational jet fighter. It was much faster than Allied piston-engine fighters. Fortunately for the Allies, production problems and shortages of materials meant the Me 262 arrived too late and in too few numbers to change the war's outcome. Britain also developed a jet plane, the Gloster Meteor, which entered service near the end of the war. The idea of a plane powered by a jet engine was revolutionary at the time. Seeing one fly would have been shocking to pilots used to older propeller-driven airplanes.

Rocket Science: V-1 and V-2

One of Germany's most famous secret projects was the development of the V-weapons. The V-1 was a flying bomb, often called a "buzz bomb" or "doodlebug," because of the loud noise its small jet engine made. It was launched from ramps and traveled at high speed toward targets like London. If the engine cut out, people below only had seconds to take cover before the bomb fell to the ground and exploded.

The V-2 rocket was even more advanced. It was the first ballistic missile ever used in war. It flew at very high altitudes and speeds, and it struck without warning because it came down faster than the speed of sound. Civilians in London and other cities had no idea a V-2 was coming until it exploded. Though these rockets caused terror and destruction, they were also expensive and hard to produce in large numbers. Still, they were a scary glimpse into the future of warfare.

Giant Tanks and Odd Vehicles

Germany also explored building giant tanks. One design was called the Maus ("Mouse"), which was ironic since it was extremely large and heavy. However, it was slow and used a huge amount of fuel. Only a couple of prototypes were made, and they never saw combat. The Soviets also tested strange tank ideas, like multi-turreted tanks that could fire in several directions at once. These designs often proved unwieldy, and the simpler T-34 tank became the backbone of the Soviet armored forces.

In Britain, there were weird inventions like the "Great Panjandrum," a huge wheel packed with explosives that was supposed to roll up onto beaches and blow up enemy defenses. In tests, the wheel wobbled and spun out of control, sometimes coming back toward the people who launched it! Because of these problems, it was never used in actual battle.

Chemical and Biological Weapons Fears

World War I had seen the use of poison gas, like chlorine and mustard gas. Many people worried that World War II would also see widespread chemical warfare. Both the Allies and the Axis stockpiled chemical weapons—like mustard gas and other deadly substances—but they hesitated to use them, fearing retaliation. Also, gas masks and protective gear had improved, making it harder to gain an advantage from chemical attacks. So, while these weapons existed, they were rarely used in combat, though the threat alone caused constant worry.

There were also rumors of biological weapons, like releasing germs or diseases. Japan's Unit 731 in China carried out terrible experiments on prisoners to see how diseases spread. These events remained secret for a long time and were only fully revealed after the war. Thankfully, large-scale biological attacks did not occur. But the fact that they were researched is a dark reminder of how far some nations were willing to go.

The Manhattan Project and Atomic Bomb Research

One of the most secret and game-changing projects of the war was the Manhattan Project, the American-led effort to develop an atomic bomb. Scientists from Europe and the United States worked together in labs spread across several locations in the U.S. They knew that if Germany or Japan built such a bomb first, the war could end very badly for the Allies. The Manhattan Project succeeded in producing the first atomic bombs by 1945. These bombs were eventually dropped on Hiroshima and Nagasaki in Japan, leading to Japan's surrender. While the atomic bomb ended the war in the Pacific, it also began a new era of nuclear fears for the world.

Decoys, Inflatable Tanks, and Fake Armies

Technology was not only about better weapons. It was also about fooling the enemy. One of the clever tactics the Allies used was creating fake armies. This involved inflating large rubber tanks, trucks, and even fake airplanes that looked real from the air. These decoys were positioned in fields with tracks made to look like real tank treads. The goal was to trick German reconnaissance aircraft into believing that the Allies had massed forces in one spot, while the real army was elsewhere.

For example, before the D-Day invasion in 1944, the Allies used fake radio traffic and inflatable tanks to make the Germans think an invasion would come near Calais in France, rather than in Normandy. This deception was critical to the success of the real invasion. Germany kept divisions near Calais because they believed that was the main target, which helped the Allies secure the beaches at Normandy.

Spy Gadgets and Hidden Tools

Spies played a major role in World War II. They carried tiny cameras and special gadgets to hide messages or poison. The British spy agency, known as MI6, worked with the Special Operations Executive (SOE) to design all sorts of hidden tools, including miniature pistols, hollow coins, and even exploding pens. Some spies carried papers with invisible ink. Others used codes hidden in ordinary letters or even in drawings of crossword puzzles.

The Americans had their own intelligence agency called the Office of Strategic Services (OSS), which later evolved into the CIA after the war. They also made unusual gadgets, like disguised explosives and secret radios that could fit into a suitcase. These devices might seem like they come from a spy movie, but they were very real at the time. With entire armies and huge battlefronts, small secret operations might not seem like a big deal, but a single spy with the right information could tip the balance in a key battle.

Weird Animal Projects

It might sound strange, but there were also attempts to use animals in warfare. For example, the Soviets tried to train dogs to run under German tanks with explosives strapped to their backs. The idea was that the dog would detonate the charge under the tank. However, this plan often failed because the dogs were frightened by engine noise or gunfire. The animals sometimes ran back to their own lines, creating a dangerous situation.

The United States explored the idea of "bat bombs." Bats would be fitted with tiny incendiary devices and released over cities in Japan. The bats would roost in buildings, and the devices would set fires. Although tested, the project was never fully deployed. Britain thought about using pigeons to guide bombs or to carry messages across enemy lines. Pigeons were indeed used to carry messages, and some became war heroes by delivering vital information when other methods failed.

Japanese Balloon Bombs

One of the strangest weapons used in the war were the Japanese balloon bombs. Japan launched large hydrogen balloons fitted with explosives. They were designed to ride high-altitude winds across the Pacific Ocean and drop bombs on North America. A few of these balloons actually landed in the United States and Canada. Some exploded, causing small fires in forests or farmland. Luckily, they did not do much damage. However, they did create fear among civilians who never expected bombs could float across the ocean. The United States government tried to keep news of the balloon bombs secret, so the Japanese would not know if the bombs were working.

Secret Plans and Operations

Along with strange inventions, there were many secret plans during World War II. Some of these plans were never used, while others were carried out in total secrecy until after the war.

- **Operation Mincemeat (British Deception Plan):** The British took a dead body, dressed it in an officer's uniform, and filled the pockets with fake letters suggesting an Allied invasion of Greece. They then set the body adrift off the coast of Spain. German agents found the body and believed the letters were real. This deception helped the Allies land in Sicily, Italy, with less resistance.

- **Operation Fortitude (D-Day Deception):** As mentioned before, this plan involved inflatable tanks, fake radio messages, and phony signals to make the Germans think the invasion would happen in Pas-de-Calais instead of Normandy. The Germans fell for it and kept troops away from the actual landing sites.

- **Soviet Maskirovka (Camouflage and Deception):** The Soviet Union had a long tradition of "maskirovka," which means camouflage or masking in warfare. During World War II, they built dummy airfields with fake planes. They moved real tanks at night and replaced them with wooden models during the day to hide their movements.

Collaboration with Scientists and Inventors

Not all strange ideas came directly from governments. Sometimes, well-known inventors and scientists offered wild ideas or were recruited. For instance, the famous American inventor Nikola Tesla was approached for thoughts on advanced weapons, although many of his ideas remained theoretical. In Britain, inventor Barnes Wallis created the "bouncing bomb," which skipped on water to destroy dams in the Ruhr area of Germany. The success of the "Dambusters Raid" showed that even unusual weapon designs could have real effects if done correctly.

In the Soviet Union, they explored all sorts of designs for better tanks, planes, and artillery. Some projects never went beyond small prototypes. The country had many engineers who worked in harsh conditions, sometimes moving entire factories east to avoid the German advance. Even under intense pressure, these engineers found ways to improve the T-34 tank and other weapons that helped defeat German forces on the Eastern Front.

The Limits of Strange Technology

While many amazing projects and inventions came to life in World War II, not all of them worked well. Some were too expensive, too complicated, or simply too odd to be practical. As the war went on, it often came down to reliable, mass-produced weapons rather than experimental ones. For example, Germany's advanced jet aircraft, rockets, and giant tanks could not stop the onslaught of the Allied armies because they were produced in far smaller numbers and often arrived too late.

In contrast, the United States poured resources into building thousands of B-17 and B-24 bombers and large fleets of ships. The Soviet Union churned out countless T-34 tanks. Britain stuck with reliable designs for its Spitfires and Hurricanes, refining them but not rushing into untested technology. These standard weapons, produced in vast quantities, ended up deciding many of the major battles.

CHAPTER 4

Unbelievable Missions Behind Enemy Lines

World War II was not just a series of giant battles. Many key actions took place in secret, far behind the front lines. Special teams or lone individuals slipped into enemy territory to gather information, carry out sabotage, or rescue important figures. Some of these missions were so daring that they sound like movie plots. Yet they were very real and often made a big difference in the outcome of the war. In this chapter, we will look at some of the most remarkable undercover operations and commando raids carried out by both the Allies and the Axis powers.

The Role of Special Forces

The idea of creating special military units to handle tricky operations started well before World War II, but it grew much bigger during the conflict. Countries like Britain set up units such as the Special Air Service (SAS) and the Special Boat Service (SBS). The United States had the Office of Strategic Services (OSS), and later special forces groups in the Army and Navy. These teams trained for missions like gathering intelligence, destroying bridges or supply depots, and even capturing high-value targets.

Germany had its own special missions, often led by bold soldiers who found ways to infiltrate enemy lines using disguises or fast-moving gliders. In the Soviet Union, "partisan" fighters operated behind German lines, cutting railways and attacking convoys. No matter which side they fought for, these special operations shared one thing: they were high-risk, high-reward. A single commando raid could disrupt an entire battle plan or force the enemy to divert large numbers of troops.

Operation Gunnerside: The Heavy Water Sabotage

One of the most famous behind-enemy-lines missions was Operation Gunnerside in Norway. The Germans were trying to produce heavy water at a plant in Vemork, Norway, which was essential for their nuclear research. If Germany succeeded, it might have helped them build an atomic weapon.

A small group of Norwegian commandos trained in Britain, then parachuted into the frozen wilderness of Norway. They had to ski across snow-covered mountains and hide in remote cabins, surviving on limited food in brutal winter conditions. After linking up with another team, they waited for the right moment to strike.

Under the cover of night, they slipped into the Vemork plant. Avoiding guards, they placed explosives on the heavy water production equipment and set the charges. When the bombs went off, the machinery was destroyed, and the Germans' nuclear research was set back. The commandos escaped into the mountains, where they faced a tough journey to safety. This mission has been called one of the most successful acts of sabotage in World War II.

The SAS in North Africa

The British Special Air Service (SAS) made a name for itself in the deserts of North Africa. Small teams in jeeps drove behind German and Italian lines at night. They would sneak up on enemy airfields, plant bombs on parked aircraft, and then speed away before the guards could react. Because the desert offered few places to hide, stealth and speed were critical.

These raids destroyed many enemy planes on the ground, weakening Axis air power. They also forced the Germans and Italians to use more soldiers to guard their bases, which took troops away from the front lines. The SAS in North Africa became legendary for their daring and unconventional tactics, showing that a handful of highly trained fighters could disrupt large formations if they used surprise to their advantage.

Otto Skorzeny and the Rescue of Mussolini

Germany also had its share of unbelievable missions. One of the most famous involved Otto Skorzeny, a German commando officer who carried out the daring rescue of Italian dictator Benito Mussolini in 1943. After Italy surrendered, Mussolini was removed from power by his own people and held captive in a hotel at the top of a mountain plateau called Gran Sasso.

Using gliders, Skorzeny and his team landed near the hotel. They caught the guards by surprise, and without firing many shots, they managed to free Mussolini. Then they flew him out in a small plane, right under the noses of Italian troops. This operation made Skorzeny a celebrity in Germany and shocked the Allies. It showed that even high-security prisoners could be rescued if attackers used speed, bold planning, and the element of surprise.

The Cockleshell Heroes: Raiding Bordeaux

In December 1942, a group of British Royal Marines carried out a mission called Operation Frankton. These marines used small collapsible canoes, nicknamed "cockles," to paddle up the Gironde estuary in France toward the port of Bordeaux. The Germans used Bordeaux to ship supplies to and from their U-boat bases. The idea was to blow up the cargo ships with limpet mines (magnetic explosives attached to a ship's hull below the waterline).

The Marines paddled at night, braving strong currents and freezing temperatures. If caught, they would face almost certain death. After reaching their targets, they attached the limpet mines and slipped away. Several ships were damaged or sunk, which disrupted German supply lines. Unfortunately, most of the raiders were captured or died during the escape. Only two men made it back to Britain. Still, the mission proved that even a small team in tiny boats could strike a heavily defended port.

French Resistance and the SOE

Behind enemy lines in France, the British Special Operations Executive (SOE) worked closely with the French Resistance. The SOE dropped agents into occupied France by parachute or by landing small planes at night in remote fields. These agents brought radios, weapons, and explosives to help local Resistance groups. They organized sabotage missions against German factories, railways, and communication lines.

One famous SOE agent was Violette Szabo, a young woman who carried out missions in France. She helped coordinate Resistance attacks and passed on vital intelligence about German troop movements. Sadly, she was caught and later executed by the Germans. Despite such risks, many SOE agents and Resistance fighters kept working behind enemy lines, tying up German forces and preparing the way for the D-Day invasion.

Partisan Warfare in Eastern Europe

The Soviet Union, Yugoslavia, and other parts of Eastern Europe also had large partisan movements. These partisans were fighters who hid in forests, mountains, or swamps and carried out guerrilla attacks on German forces. They blew up bridges, ambushed supply convoys, and helped Allied pilots who had been shot down. Because the Eastern Front was vast, the Germans struggled to control every area.

In Yugoslavia, partisans led by Josip Broz Tito fought against the Axis for years. They set up hidden camps and hospitals in remote regions, using knowledge of the terrain to avoid capture. At times, they even liberated small towns, holding them until German forces arrived in strength. Their efforts forced the Axis to commit more divisions, which meant fewer troops could go to other fronts.

Unusual Undercover Work in Asia

In Asia, the war brought together a mix of Allied forces and local fighters. The British organized groups like the Chindits, led by Orde Wingate, who marched deep behind Japanese lines in Burma. They aimed to disrupt Japanese supply routes, destroy bridges, and set up bases in the jungle. Conditions were harsh, with deadly diseases like malaria and dysentery claiming many lives. Yet these operations kept the Japanese off balance and supported the main Allied offensives from India into Burma.

The American-led OSS also worked in China and Southeast Asia, training local guerrillas to fight the Japanese. Using radios and small arms, these groups gathered intelligence on Japanese troop movements. Sometimes they guided American bombers to hidden Japanese bases. Conditions in the jungles were tough, with monsoon rains and limited supplies. But their efforts helped weaken Japanese control over vast territories.

Operation Chariot: The St. Nazaire Raid

Another incredible British mission was Operation Chariot in 1942. The target was the French port of St. Nazaire, where the Germans had a large dry dock that could repair big battleships like the Tirpitz. The British feared that if the Tirpitz ever needed repairs, it could use St. Nazaire as a safe haven.

To stop this, British commandos rammed an old destroyer packed with explosives right into the dock gates. The plan was for the commandos to get off the ship, plant more explosives, and destroy as much of the dock as they could. Many commandos died or were captured, but the massive charge on the destroyer eventually exploded, wrecking the dock and making it unusable for the rest of the war. Even though the raid was costly, it removed a major threat to Allied shipping in the Atlantic.

Glider Missions and Night Drops

Flying behind enemy lines was very dangerous. Gliders—planes without engines—were sometimes used because they made less noise and could land in smaller spaces. For example, during the invasion of Normandy, the British used gliders to land near Pegasus Bridge. Their surprise arrival helped secure key bridges over the Caen Canal and the Orne River. This prevented German tanks from reaching the beaches quickly.

Such glider missions required a lot of skill from pilots. Once they released from a towing aircraft, they had only one chance to land safely. If the landing zone was filled with trees or the enemy spotted them, the mission could fail right away. Despite these risks, glider operations were used several times during the war, including in the famous Operation Market Garden in the Netherlands.

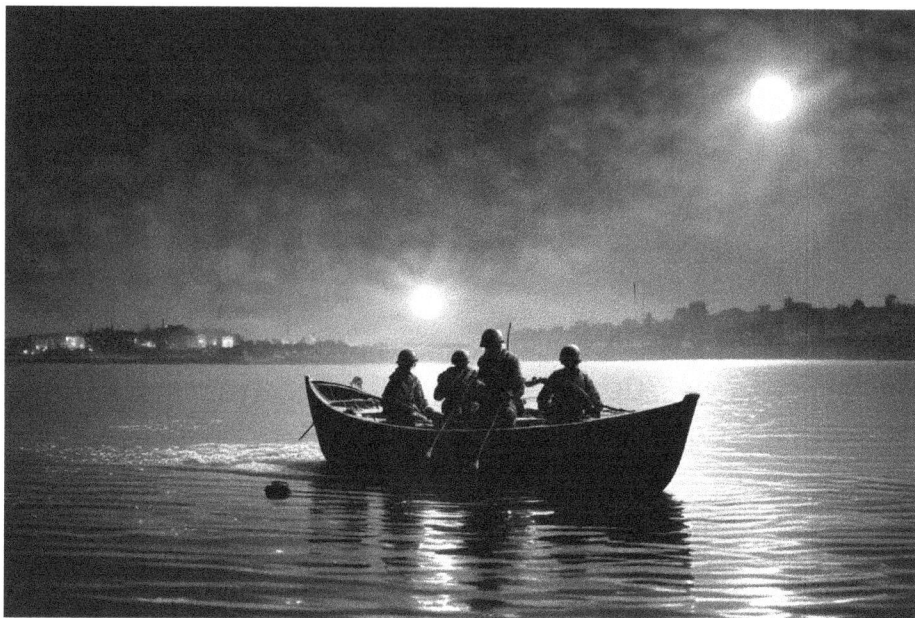

Espionage and Double Agents

Some missions behind enemy lines did not involve guns at all—they were about gathering secrets. Many spies lived under false identities in occupied cities, pretending to be locals or even collaborating with the enemy. In truth, they were sending coded messages to Allied headquarters, warning them of troop movements, weapon deployments, and other plans.

One of the most famous double agents was Juan Pujol García, known by the codename "Garbo." He fed false information to the Germans, making them believe he was loyal to the Axis. In reality, he worked for the British. His fake network of spies reported that the main Allied invasion would come at Calais, not Normandy. This deception kept German units away from the real beaches during D-Day.

Small Incidents, Big Impacts

Not every behind-enemy-lines mission was a large operation. Sometimes, individuals took great risks with surprising results. A single soldier or local resident might sneak out of an occupied city to hand over a map or a list of enemy locations. Another might cut telephone lines at just the right moment, delaying an important message and changing the outcome of a battle. These small acts of courage, repeated many times across different fronts, added up to a big difference.

The Human Cost

While these missions were brave and thrilling, they were also very dangerous. Many commandos and spies were captured, tortured, or executed. Civilians who helped them risked not just their own lives but also their families. In Nazi-occupied countries, punishments for helping Allied agents were severe. Still, people kept doing it because they believed in fighting against oppression.

In some areas, special operatives befriended local villagers who supported them with food, shelter, and information. This goodwill was crucial for success. Without local help, Allied spies and commandos behind enemy lines would have struggled to survive. These stories show that regular people, not just trained soldiers, played a vital part in the war's outcome.

Axis Missions Behind Allied Lines

It was not only the Allies who carried out daring missions. Germany, Italy, and Japan also had spies and special forces who tried to gather intelligence and disrupt Allied operations. For example, German U-boats sometimes dropped agents on American or Canadian shores. Their mission was to blend into the population and sabotage factories or railroads. However, many of these Axis agents were caught quickly because they stood out or made mistakes with local customs.

In North Africa, German reconnaissance units sometimes drove deep behind Allied lines to report on troop movements. They relied on desert navigation skills and radio equipment. A few even used captured Allied vehicles to trick sentries. Italy's Decima Flottiglia MAS used "human torpedoes" and frogmen to attack British ships in Mediterranean harbors. These frogmen would ride slow-moving torpedoes underwater, attach explosives to enemy ships, and slip away. They sank or damaged several Allied vessels with these daring techniques.

Lessons Learned

These unbelievable missions behind enemy lines taught militaries a lot about tactics and strategy. Speed, surprise, and good intelligence often mattered more than large numbers of soldiers. It also showed that air power and naval power alone could not guarantee victory if the enemy was able to sneak small teams in for sabotage. In future wars, special operations forces would continue to play a major role, building on the lessons learned in World War II.

The Legacy of Special Operations

After the war, many of the units that carried out these operations were kept or expanded. For example, Britain maintained the SAS, and the United States formed new special forces in the Army, Navy, and other branches. The tactics developed in World War II—from dropping spies at night to using stealthy raids—became the foundation of special operations in later conflicts.

The brave men and women who risked their lives behind enemy lines are remembered as heroes. Their stories remind us that big battles are not the only way wars are fought. Sometimes, a small group with a daring plan can do more damage than a large army if they strike the right target at the right time.

Moving Forward

In the next chapters, we will look at other surprising sides of the war. There are stories about animals that served in the military, strange strategies tried on both sides, and moments where small mistakes led to huge consequences. World War II was so large that even with massive armies clashing, there was still plenty of room for bizarre twists and unexpected heroes.

The missions behind enemy lines stand out because they required so much courage and cunning. From sabotaging heavy water plants in Norway to rescuing leaders held captive, these operations add a layer of excitement and intrigue to the history of the war. They remind us that creativity, daring, and human willpower can shine in the darkest times.

CHAPTER 5

Animals in Service and Bizarre Strategies

World War II was the largest and most complex war in history. Countries turned to every possible resource to gain an advantage. This included calling on various animals to help soldiers on land, at sea, and in the air. At first, the idea of using animals might sound odd, but in the pressure of war, people often tried creative or unusual strategies. Alongside these animal stories, there were many strange plans and tactics that nations came up with. In this chapter, we will explore the role animals played and some of the bizarre strategies that were tested during the war years.

Animals on the Battlefield

During World War I, horses, mules, and carrier pigeons were common sights. Although technology had advanced greatly by World War II—tanks, trucks, and radios were widespread—animals still proved useful in many situations.

Horses and Mules

Even though Germany used tanks and trucks in its blitzkrieg attacks, horses and mules were still essential for transporting supplies in rough terrain. In areas like the Soviet Union, muddy roads or freezing conditions made motor vehicles useless. Horses could pull wagons and artillery through thick mud or snow.

Germany famously used millions of horses during the invasion of the Soviet Union, because their supply lines stretched over huge distances and machines were not always reliable in extreme weather. The Soviet army also depended on horses for cavalry and transport, especially early in the war before their factories produced enough trucks and tanks.

Dogs

Dogs served as messengers, guard dogs, and even search and rescue helpers on battlefields. In the Pacific, some American soldiers used dogs to detect hidden enemy fighters in the thick jungle.

The Soviet Union tried to train "anti-tank" dogs. These dogs were fitted with explosives and taught to run underneath enemy tanks, where a trigger would set off the bomb. However, this plan often failed because the dogs were frightened by gunfire or sometimes ran back to their own lines. It was a sad example of desperate measures in warfare.

Carrier Pigeons

Although radios were common in World War II, they could break down, be intercepted, or run out of batteries. Carrier pigeons provided a backup method of communication.

One famous pigeon named "G.I. Joe" saved the lives of many Allied soldiers in Italy by carrying a critical message that stopped friendly planes from bombing a location the Allies had just captured. Without the pigeon's fast delivery, the bombing run might have harmed Allied troops.

Another pigeon, called "Cher Ami" (though more famous for World War I), showed how birds could be wounded in flight but still deliver messages.

Cats at Sea

On many ships, cats served as mousers to keep rats away from food supplies and wiring. Some cats became mascots for their ship's crew, bringing a bit of comfort in the tense conditions of naval warfare.

There is a story about a cat named "Unsinkable Sam" (though some argue about the truth). Allegedly, this cat survived the sinking of three different ships: a German battleship (Bismarck) and later two British ships. Each time, the cat was found floating on some debris and rescued. Real or not, the tale illustrates how seamen valued feline companions.

Dolphins and Sea Lions?

Rumors persist that both Allied and Axis powers considered training dolphins or sea lions for harbor defense, though details are hard to verify. The idea was to have them detect submarines or underwater mines. Most of these plans either stayed in the experimental stage or were too difficult to carry out effectively during the war.

Strange Airborne Projects Involving Animals

While traditional uses of animals were common, some attempts were far more unusual:

Bat Bombs

The United States experimented with a concept called the "bat bomb." Tiny incendiary bombs were attached to bats. The bats would be released over enemy cities, then roost in buildings, setting them on fire. The plan was tested in the desert, and some test bats escaped and accidentally set part of an airbase on fire. Because the atomic bomb project (the Manhattan Project) took priority, the bat bomb idea was never fully deployed in the war.

Pigeon-Guided Missiles

Another American psychologist, B.F. Skinner, proposed training pigeons to guide bombs by pecking at a screen showing the target.

The idea, known as "Project Pigeon," was that the pigeons would keep the crosshairs centered on the target, adjusting the bomb's flight. This plan never went into battle. However, it demonstrates how creative (or bizarre) people could be when faced with the pressure of war.

Other Unusual Strategies

Animals were not the only unique or quirky resource used. Many strategies appear strange when we look back at them now:

1. **Using Icebergs and "Ice Ships"**

   ○ One plan considered by the British was called Project Habakkuk—building a giant aircraft carrier out of pykrete (a mixture of wood pulp and frozen water). The idea was that such a ship would be strong, repairable at sea, and could help supply convoys in the Atlantic. A small-scale test model was built in Canada, but the project proved too costly and complicated, and was eventually dropped.

47

2. **Operation Outward: Balloons with Wires**

    ○ Britain launched thousands of small balloons carrying long steel wires or incendiary devices to drift over Europe. The steel wires could cause short circuits if they landed on power lines, while the incendiary devices could start fires. These balloons were cheap to make and sometimes annoyed the Germans by damaging power stations. However, they never caused huge amounts of destruction.

3. **Flooding and Scorched Earth**

    ○ In some cases, armies used large-scale environmental damage to slow the enemy. The Soviet Union sometimes destroyed dams, fields, or railways as they retreated, hoping to make it harder for the Germans to operate in captured regions. China famously flooded the Yellow River to stop the advancing Japanese in 1938, though this event happened just before the full outbreak of World War II in Europe. While it slowed Japan, it also caused huge suffering for Chinese civilians.

4. **Loudspeakers and Fake Music**

    ○ Propaganda was a key tool, but sometimes armies played recordings of tank movements or loud music to confuse enemy patrols. These attempts were small-scale compared to the bigger deception operations, but they underscore the variety of "psychological warfare" tactics used during the war.

Psychological Warfare and Leaflets

Besides direct combat or sabotage, all sides used psychological warfare to lower the morale of enemy soldiers and civilians. One common method was dropping leaflets from planes. These leaflets might:

- Urge enemy troops to surrender by saying they would be treated well.
- Spread false news or gossip to create confusion.
- Show horrifying images of what might happen if one kept fighting, hoping to scare soldiers into giving up.

However, not all propaganda worked. Many people ignored the leaflets, and some became more determined to resist after seeing enemy attempts to weaken their morale. But in some cases, leaflets and broadcast messages did have an effect, especially when people were already exhausted or isolated.

Japan's Balloon Bombs Revisited

We touched on Japan's balloon bombs in a previous chapter, but they are worth mentioning again as one of the strangest war strategies. These bombs were real weapons carried by large paper balloons. The balloons sailed across the Pacific Ocean with the help of high-altitude winds. Their goal was to start fires or cause panic in the United States and Canada. Although only a small number caused damage, they stand as an example of how creative (and desperate) warfare can become.

Operation Fantasia: Psychological Warfare with "Ghosts"

In an even stranger idea, the United States Office of Strategic Services (OSS) briefly explored a plan called "Operation Fantasia."

The idea was to use chemical or other means to convince Japanese people that their country's Shinto gods had turned against them. They hoped that sightings of a "ghostly fox," a creature with significance in Japanese folklore, might spread panic or lower morale. This plan never got off the ground, partly because it seemed too far-fetched and difficult to carry out. Yet it shows the lengths to which governments were willing to go for an advantage.

Cultural and Superstitious Tactics

Warfare often intersects with culture and superstition. Soldiers on all sides carried lucky charms, prayed for safety, or avoided certain things they saw as bad omens. In some parts of the war, rumors spread about curses or mystical powers. For instance:

- Some Allied troops believed German tanks had near-mythical strength. These fears could harm morale until they realized the tanks were vulnerable to well-placed anti-tank weapons.
- Stories circulated among Japanese soldiers about certain Allied guns or bombs having supernatural effects, which sometimes made them more cautious in battle.
- In North Africa, both Allied and Axis troops faced local legends about desert spirits or cursed relics. Such beliefs rarely changed actual battle outcomes, but they added another layer of stress or superstition.

Extreme Measures: Suicide Missions

When a war becomes desperate, some forces turn to suicidal or near-suicidal attacks:

- **Kamikaze Pilots**: In the final years of the war, Japan used kamikaze pilots who crashed their planes directly into enemy ships. This caused severe damage to Allied vessels in the Pacific. The idea was that sacrificing a pilot and a plane was worthwhile if it guaranteed the sinking or damaging of a large ship. Many kamikaze missions failed due to Allied fighter planes or anti-aircraft fire. Still, they left a psychological effect on Allied sailors who had to watch for any plane diving toward them.
- **Human Torpedoes**: The Italian Decima Flottiglia MAS (and also Japan) used manned torpedoes to sneak into harbors and attach explosives to ships. These missions were extremely risky. Although not strictly "suicide missions," the odds of survival were quite low.

These acts remind us that war can push human beings to the most extreme decisions, often fueled by national pride, propaganda, or a sense of duty.

Animal Mascots and Morale

On a lighter note, many units and ships adopted animal mascots to boost morale. These mascots had no direct strategic value, but they provided comfort and entertainment. Examples include:

- **Wojtek the Bear**: A famous case is the Polish Army's use of a brown bear named Wojtek. He was acquired as a cub by soldiers in the Middle East. Wojtek became a beloved mascot and even helped carry shells during the Battle of Monte Cassino. After the war, he was taken to a zoo in Scotland, where former soldiers would visit him.

- **Other Critters**: Soldiers kept dogs, goats, monkeys, and even birds as pets in their camps. Such animals relieved stress, offered companionship, and reminded soldiers of home.

These stories show a softer side of military life, demonstrating how troops tried to stay positive in very difficult times.

Why Such Bizarre Strategies?

People often wonder why nations resorted to strategies that seem so strange or even silly today. There are several reasons:

1. **Desperation**: In total war, every idea might be considered if it could bring victory or avoid defeat.
2. **Rapid Technology Growth**: With the technology boom of the 1930s and 1940s, many new scientific ideas were untested. This sparked wild projects that mixed science and wishful thinking.

3. **Limited Knowledge**: Nations lacked the quick communication we have today. Military leaders sometimes made decisions based on incomplete or false information, leading them to try outlandish projects.
4. **Propaganda Value**: Some strange ideas could be exaggerated to scare the enemy. Just hearing rumors of a "bat bomb" or an "ice ship" might cause worry or confusion.

Long-Term Impact

Some bizarre tactics, like kamikaze attacks, left lasting impressions on military thinking. They showed that a determined force could still inflict serious damage, even if technically outmatched. Others, like the attempt to use animals in highly specialized roles, had less impact but remain a curious footnote in the history of warfare. In modern times, using animals such as dogs for bomb detection or rescue missions continues, but the extreme measures of turning them into living weapons have mostly ended.

As for the large deception plans and psychological warfare, many of these ideas developed further after the war, forming the basis of modern special operations and propaganda strategies. Today's militaries still study World War II for lessons on human creativity, desperation, and the boundaries of what soldiers and nations might try when facing a massive conflict.

CHAPTER 6

Miscommunications and Lucky Escapes

War is unpredictable. Even with the best planning, things can go wrong—or strangely right. In World War II, mistakes sometimes led to entire units being in the wrong place at the right time, or commanders attacking the wrong targets. At other times, chance happenings allowed soldiers to evade capture or survive situations that seemed hopeless. In this chapter, we will explore notable miscommunications and lucky escapes that shaped the war in surprising ways.

The Fog of War

"Fog of war" is a term used to describe the uncertainty and confusion that comes with any large battle or campaign. On the battlefield, soldiers often rely on quick messages, radio signals, or even hand gestures. Orders get lost or garbled. Technology fails. People get tired and stressed. All these factors create conditions where misunderstandings can easily occur. Let's look at some memorable examples from World War II.

Dunkirk's Strange Delays

One of the early lucky escapes of the war happened at Dunkirk in 1940, when hundreds of thousands of Allied soldiers were cornered by the German army on the beaches of northern France. The

Germans seemed on the verge of a decisive victory. Then, for reasons that are still debated, Hitler ordered his tank units to halt outside Dunkirk for a short period. This pause gave the Allies enough time to organize a massive evacuation by sea. Over 300,000 Allied soldiers were rescued, many by small civilian boats.

Why did Hitler hesitate? Some think he wanted the Luftwaffe to handle the destruction of the Allied forces. Others say he worried about his tanks getting stuck in the marshy terrain. Regardless, this delay was a miscommunication or miscalculation that changed the course of the war. Britain kept its army, allowing it to fight on.

Italy's Surprises in Greece

When Italy invaded Greece in 1940, Benito Mussolini believed his forces would quickly occupy the country. Instead, the Greek army fought back fiercely. Italian units were not well-coordinated, and supplies ran out. There are accounts of Italian generals receiving unclear orders or ignoring them. Some divisions advanced when they should have retreated, and others retreated when they were supposed to hold their ground. As a result, the Greeks pushed the Italians back.

This was an embarrassing setback for Mussolini. Germany later had to invade Greece to support its Italian ally, which forced Hitler to delay his plans to invade the Soviet Union. That delay, in turn, led to the Germans hitting the Russian winter at a more dangerous time. So a series of miscommunications and underestimating the Greeks had a ripple effect on the entire war.

The Myth of the "Panzers on the Wrong Road"

During the Battle of France, the French expected German tanks to move in a straightforward way, so they positioned their defenses accordingly. Instead, the Germans went through the Ardennes Forest, which was considered impassable by large tank units. Part of the success of this plan was that French generals received conflicting reports. Some believed the Germans were heading north, others thought they were stuck in the forest. By the time the truth was clear, it was too late to stop the German blitzkrieg.

These mistaken assumptions or poor communications allowed the Germans to strike the French rear and flank, leading to the rapid fall of France. Sometimes, just a few hours' delay in responding to critical information can make all the difference in a fast-moving war.

The Battle of Midway: Misread Signals

In the Pacific, the Battle of Midway in 1942 was a turning point. Japanese admirals planned to lure the U.S. Navy into a trap near Midway Atoll. However, American codebreakers had deciphered enough of Japan's messages to guess their plan. A small but important example of confusion came when the Japanese used the code designation "AF" for a target. The Americans suspected "AF" meant Midway, but they needed proof. So they sent a fake radio message from Midway saying they were short on fresh water. Soon after, the Americans intercepted Japanese chatter saying that "AF" was low on water. This confirmed that Midway was the target.

Because the Japanese believed they still had the element of surprise, they were caught off guard. The U.S. Navy's dive-bombers sank four Japanese aircraft carriers. Had the Japanese realized their code was broken, they might have changed their plans and avoided disaster.

Confusion at Pearl Harbor

Japan's attack on Pearl Harbor in December 1941 was a surprise to most Americans. But there were signs—misread signals and overlooked hints—that could have warned the U.S. in time to mount a better defense. For instance:

- A radar station on Oahu detected the incoming Japanese planes, but the report was dismissed, possibly because an officer assumed they were American B-17 bombers arriving from the mainland.
- Diplomatic messages between the U.S. and Japan had been growing tense, but no one fully expected an attack on Pearl Harbor.
- Some intelligence suggested Japan might strike somewhere in the Pacific, but Pearl Harbor was not at the top of the list of likely targets.

These misunderstandings and assumptions left the U.S. Navy unprepared on the morning of December 7, 1941. The attack severely damaged the Pacific Fleet, though the aircraft carriers were luckily at sea and escaped harm.

Friendly Fire Incidents

Miscommunication sometimes led to tragic "friendly fire" events, where allies fired on their own side by mistake:

- In the confusion of night battles or poor weather, planes and ships sometimes shot at friendly units. This happened in various theaters of war, including the Atlantic, the Mediterranean, and the Pacific.
- On D-Day, some Allied bombers dropped their loads too short, hitting Allied troops on the beaches instead of German defenses. Dense smoke, shifting winds, and timing errors contributed to this heartbreaking mistake.

These incidents underline how easily chaos can arise in the middle of battle, despite training and planning.

Operation Market Garden: Too Ambitious

In September 1944, the Allies launched Operation Market Garden, an airborne operation meant to capture a series of bridges in the Netherlands, leading to a quick advance into Germany. British and American paratroopers landed behind enemy lines to secure these bridges. However, the plan depended on everything going perfectly. German resistance was stronger than expected, and some of the drop zones were too far from the bridges.

Communication problems made things worse. Radios failed to work in certain areas, and supply drops landed in German-held territory. The Allies eventually lost the battle for the crucial bridge at Arnhem. Many blamed the defeat on poor intelligence, overconfidence, and the breakdown of radio communications among scattered parachute units. This became a famous example of how a bold plan can collapse if the details are not managed well.

Lucky "Friendly" Arrests

Sometimes, a mistake led to unexpected benefits. Consider the story of a British spy who parachuted into France but landed off course. Local people mistook him for a German spy and nearly turned him over to the Germans. But after a heated discussion, the townsfolk realized he was an Allied agent. They hid him instead, and he was able to gather crucial information on German troop movements. Had they handed him over, his mission would have failed. Instead, the "friendly" arrest saved his life and allowed him to carry out important work.

Running into the Enemy … and Running Away

War tales are full of strange encounters where small groups of soldiers ran into each other by accident—sometimes with odd results:

- A German patrol might stumble upon a British patrol in the dark. Both sides, startled, fired a few shots, then quickly withdrew in confusion. Neither side realized how few the enemy really were.

- On the Eastern Front, Soviet partisans and German foraging parties might cross paths in a forest. If neither group was prepared, they might both retreat rather than risk a fight without knowing the other's strength.

These minor incidents rarely changed the course of the war, but they highlight how uncertainty and fear can rule the night in a conflict zone.

The Capture of Vital Documents by Accident

There are times when sheer luck led to vital intelligence falling into the right hands:

- A German officer carrying important invasion plans got lost in bad weather, landed his plane in neutral Belgium by mistake, and was arrested. The Allies gained knowledge of Germany's upcoming moves, which helped them prepare.
- An Allied courier left a briefcase in a café, and a curious local nearly opened it. Fortunately, someone realized the mistake, and the documents were retrieved before enemy agents could see them. If the briefcase had been lost, key Allied plans might have been exposed.

Such stories show that the simplest human errors can have huge effects during wartime.

Lucky Escapes from POW Camps

Many prisoners of war (POWs) attempted daring escapes, and sometimes luck played a big part:

- **The Great Escape (Stalag Luft III)**: A famous mass escape from a German POW camp. British, Canadian, and other Allied airmen dug tunnels under the camp fences. They used scavenged materials, homemade tools, and even built ventilation systems. Although most escapees were recaptured, a few made it to freedom. The entire operation was very risky, and small strokes of luck—like guards not noticing suspicious dirt—kept it going.
- **Italian and German POW Camps**: Some Allied soldiers bribed guards or tricked them with fake IDs to leave. Others used the chaos during Allied bombing raids to flee. Many who escaped were helped by local resistance groups. A single wrong turn or minor mix-up could have led to capture, but good fortune sometimes sided with the escapers.

The Role of Weather and Coincidence

Mother Nature also played a role in causing miscommunications and unexpected outcomes:

- Storms in the English Channel forced the postponement of D-Day from June 5 to June 6, 1944. Bad weather also made the Germans believe no attack would come, so many of their officers were away from their posts. This timing error gave the Allies a slight edge.
- In the Soviet Union, the mud seasons (rasputitsa) turned roads into swamps, slowing German armored advances. This allowed Soviet forces to regroup. German generals often complained about receiving incomplete weather reports or not expecting the terrain to become so impassable.

These natural factors combined with human confusion to shape battles in unpredictable ways.

Small Translation Errors with Big Consequences

When armies composed of different nationalities fought side by side, translation errors caused confusion:

- Allied forces included Americans, British, Canadians, Free French, Poles, and others. Commanders sometimes misread each other's signals due to language barriers. Orders might be misunderstood or not passed on correctly.
- On the Axis side, German and Italian units had trouble coordinating. Italians might get instructions from Germans that were unclear or poorly translated. As a result, attacks were not well synchronized, leading to defeat in some battles.

These misunderstandings might seem minor, but in the heat of battle, a delay of even an hour could mean the difference between success and failure.

When Spies Are Not Believed

Another strange part of miscommunication is when accurate intelligence is ignored:

- The Soviet Union had spies warning that Germany planned to invade in June 1941, but Stalin refused to believe it. Some say he thought Hitler would never break the Molotov-Ribbentrop Pact so soon. As a result, Soviet defenses were caught off guard when Operation Barbarossa began.
- British intelligence sometimes doubted reports from local French or Polish sources, assuming the sources might be compromised or exaggerating. This occasionally caused missed opportunities to strike or defend more effectively.

Paranoia and mistrust can lead to ignoring good information, showing that sometimes it is not just about receiving messages but also believing them.

Lucky Shots and Narrow Escapes

Individual soldiers or small units often told stories of "one-in-a-million" events:

- A single bullet might knock out a tank's engine through a small vent.
- A shell could fail to explode upon impact, saving the lives of those nearby.
- Pilots recounted returning to base with planes riddled with holes, yet they managed to land safely.

While these stories did not always shape grand strategy, they shaped morale. Hearing about a friend's miraculous survival gave hope to others.

Changing History Through Miscommunication

Could the war have ended differently if certain messages were received or understood correctly? Possibly. Miscommunication is part of human nature, and in a giant conflict like World War II, countless moving parts made errors inevitable. Yet these errors and lucky escapes highlight the role of chance in war. A single misunderstanding might lead to a crucial bridge being left undefended or an entire division moving to the wrong location.

We often think of World War II in terms of well-planned operations and large battles. But the personal, human side—the side where people get lost, mix up orders, or get a lucky break—is equally important. Wars are fought by real people, and real people make mistakes.

CHAPTER 7

The Ghost Armies and Deception Tactics

During World War II, battles were often won or lost by more than just brute force. Information and deception played a huge role. Armies worked hard to fool their enemies about where they would attack or how big their forces were. This chapter explores how both Allied and Axis powers used clever tricks, from inflatable tanks to staged radio calls, creating "ghost" armies that never really existed. These tactics saved lives, changed strategies, and, in some cases, sped up the end of the war.

The Importance of Deception

World War II was a global conflict involving massive armies, navies, and air forces. While technology like radar and codebreaking changed how countries gathered intelligence, old-fashioned deception still proved useful. If one side could convince the enemy that tanks were gathering in one place—while the real armor massed somewhere else—they could gain a huge advantage. By the time the enemy realized the truth, it might be too late.

Some armies had specialized units tasked only with creating illusions. They would build fake structures, use recorded sounds, and spread false reports over the radio. For the opposing side, trying to figure out what was real and what was fake became much harder.

Britain's Early Deception Efforts

Before the United States entered the war, Britain was already developing ways to mislead German intelligence. One early trick was to use "dummy" airplanes, made of wood or canvas, set up at airfields. From the air, they looked real enough to fool German reconnaissance flights. The idea was to draw enemy bombs toward these fake planes instead of hitting the real ones. Some of these decoys had small fires burning nearby to mimic the heat and exhaust of an active airstrip. German pilots might return home reporting they had destroyed a major RAF base, when in fact they had only hit dummies.

The British also used "Starfish" sites to protect cities during night bombings. These were fake target areas constructed outside major towns, lit up to resemble real streets and buildings. When German bombers flew over at night, they often dropped their bombs on these decoys instead of the actual city centers, sparing civilian lives.

German Deception Tactics

Germany also recognized the value of deception. They created phony airfields with wooden planes, just as the British did. Sometimes, the Germans placed fake tanks near the French coast to suggest an invasion of Britain could happen at any time, hoping to tie up British defenses.

In North Africa, General Erwin Rommel used camouflage nets, fake tank hulls, and even smoke generators to hide the movement of his forces. When the British tried to track German armor from the air, they were sometimes fooled by decoy vehicles. However, as the war progressed, Allied technology improved, including photo reconnaissance that could tell real armor from cardboard or wooden shapes by looking at details like tire tracks and shadows.

The Creation of the Ghost Army

The United States formed a special unit called the 23rd Headquarters Special Troops, popularly known as the "Ghost Army." Their primary job was to stage elaborate deceptions in Europe after the D-Day landings in 1944. They used three main tactics:

1. **Visual Deception**: Inflatable tanks and trucks were set up to look like an entire armored division. Soldiers would even create fake camps with laundry on the line, footprints in the dirt, and other signs of real occupation.
2. **Audio Deception**: Recordings of tanks moving, trucks driving, and construction work were played over loudspeakers that could be heard miles away. This made the enemy think large forces were gathering.
3. **Radio Deception**: Skilled radio operators sent fake messages mimicking the style and call signs of real units. German eavesdroppers would pick up these signals and assume the presence of an entire division, even though only a small group of soldiers was actually there.

These Ghost Army operations happened in secrecy for many decades after the war. The soldiers involved were artists, designers, architects, and engineers, recruited because of their creativity. Some had backgrounds in theater or advertising, which helped them stage believable illusions.

Operation Fortitude and the D-Day Landing

One of the biggest and most successful deception efforts of the entire war was Operation Fortitude, carried out by the Allies to support the D-Day invasion in June 1944. The plan had two main parts: Fortitude North (aimed at Norway) and Fortitude South (aimed at the Pas-de-Calais region in France). The goal was to keep the Germans guessing about where the real invasion would land.

- **Fortitude North**: The Allies spread rumors and staged fake troop movements indicating that a massive invasion force was gathering in Scotland to strike Norway. This kept German divisions stationed in Norway, where they posed no threat to the real invasion in France.
- **Fortitude South**: This involved creating a dummy First U.S. Army Group in southeast England. General George Patton, seen by the Germans as a top Allied commander, was placed in charge (on paper) of this fake army. The Allies set up inflatable tanks, trucks, and ships. They sent fake radio messages about troop preparations. German reconnaissance planes saw what looked like a real army massing across the English Channel from Pas-de-Calais. This fooled the Germans into thinking the main invasion would come there.

When D-Day landed in Normandy, Hitler and many German generals still believed it might be just a diversion. They kept key units in Calais, waiting for the "real" invasion that never came. This gave the Allies time to establish a beachhead in Normandy. Without Operation Fortitude, the D-Day landings might have faced much stronger resistance.

Operation Bertram in North Africa

Before the Battle of El Alamein in 1942, the British used an impressive deception plan called Operation Bertram against Rommel's Afrika Korps. The Allies built fake water pipelines and positioned dummy tanks in one sector to suggest a major assault would come there. Meanwhile, they hid real tanks in different locations, disguising them as harmless trucks or supply vehicles. They also constructed fake supply dumps, leading the Germans to believe the main attack would be delayed.

When the real offensive began, the Germans were caught off guard. They had positioned many of their forces in the wrong place, expecting an attack where the decoys had been set. This contributed to a key British victory at El Alamein, which helped turn the tide in North Africa.

The Ruses of Maskirovka (Soviet Deception)

The Soviet Union had a long tradition of **maskirovka**, which translates to "camouflage" or "deception." During World War II, the Red Army used widespread deception to trick the Germans about troop movements, supply lines, and the timing of offensives.

One example was during the Battle of Stalingrad. The Soviets secretly gathered large forces on the flanks of the city. They used camouflage and built dummy fortifications elsewhere to draw German attention away. When they launched their counteroffensive in November 1942, the Germans were unprepared for the sheer size of the Soviet armies closing in around them.

Later in the war, Soviet deceptions continued in operations to liberate other parts of Eastern Europe. By moving units only at night, using dummy tanks, and carefully guarding radio traffic, they managed to hide the direction of their assaults until it was too late for the Germans to respond effectively.

The Art of Disguise

Deception also involved using costumes, fake uniforms, and disguised vehicles in smaller missions. For example, special forces might dress in enemy uniforms to move through lines or to get close to a target. However, this was risky because being caught in the enemy's uniform could lead to execution as a spy.

Some infiltration teams used enemy vehicles that had been captured or found abandoned. They repainted them with friendly markings to sneak behind lines. While such maneuvers were not always successful, they caused confusion. If an enemy soldier saw a familiar vehicle or uniform, he might not realize danger until it was too late.

Double Agents and False Intel

Deception did not end with fake tanks and dummy airfields; it also involved human spies acting as double agents. These agents pretended to work for one side while secretly serving the other. The Allies used several famous double agents to feed misleading information to Germany. One of the most notable was **Juan Pujol García**, known as Agent Garbo. Germany believed he ran a large spy network in Britain, but in truth, he worked for British intelligence. He passed on carefully crafted lies, which supported Allied deception plans leading up to D-Day.

Similar double-cross operations existed on other fronts. The Germans, Japanese, and Soviets all tried to run double agents, though the Allies had some of the biggest successes in coordinating large-scale fake intelligence.

The Risks of Overconfidence

While deception was powerful, it could also lead to problems if one side believed its own false stories. Germany, for instance, sometimes fell victim to its own propaganda, assuming it was stronger than it really was. Some generals might ignore real intelligence because it clashed with the illusions they had already accepted.

Allied commanders, too, could be tricked by German ruses. If a scout plane reported seeing a row of tanks, officers had to decide if those tanks were real or just inflatable shapes. Mistakes in judgment could lead to wasted attacks on empty positions or poor defenses against genuine threats.

Small Deceptions with Big Impact

Not every deception was on the scale of Operation Fortitude. Sometimes even small tricks achieved results:

- **Dummy Minefields**: Engineers would place fake signs and barbed wire, making it look like an area was heavily mined. Enemy soldiers, not wanting to risk injury, would avoid those zones or move more slowly, giving defenders an advantage.
- **Fake Communications**: A single radio operator might move around, broadcasting signals from different locations to suggest a large formation was scattered across an area.
- **Decoy Soldiers**: Some units used lifelike mannequins ("Oscar") dropped from planes at night to create the illusion of parachute landings. German defenders often rushed to the drop zones, only to find dummy figures lying in the fields.

Though small, these tactics disrupted enemy plans and sometimes gave the real soldiers the edge they needed to succeed.

Lasting Lessons of Deception

The deception tactics of World War II proved how creativity and trickery could save lives and support major offensives. After the war, many nations studied these methods and included them in their military doctrines. Modern armies still use camouflage, dummy targets, and electronic jamming to confuse opponents. Although technology has advanced, the core idea remains: if you can confuse the enemy about your true intentions, you hold an advantage.

During World War II, these ghost armies, fake airfields, and staged operations often spelled the difference between victory and defeat. They also highlight the human side of warfare, where wit and cleverness can be just as crucial as firepower. In the midst of massive battles and deadly technology, a handful of soldiers pumping up inflatable tanks could alter the course of entire campaigns.

CHAPTER 8

Spies, Lies, and Codebreakers

If there was one activity during World War II that truly spanned the globe, it was espionage. Spies lurked in every major city, on every front, and within many government offices. Nations poured huge resources into codebreaking teams, who worked around the clock to crack enemy ciphers and protect their own secrets. This chapter dives into the world of secrecy, where a single decoded message or a well-placed spy could change the direction of a battle—or even the entire war.

The Art of Espionage

Espionage is the practice of using spies to gather information from an enemy or potential enemy. During World War II, espionage took many forms:

- **Human Intelligence (HUMINT)**: Agents living in enemy territory or working in important offices to gather secrets and pass them on.
- **Signals Intelligence (SIGINT)**: Listening in on enemy radio traffic and cracking coded messages.
- **Photo Reconnaissance**: Taking detailed pictures from high-flying planes. While not exactly "espionage," it often worked hand in hand with spy activities.

Spies had to be very careful. If caught, they faced harsh punishments, often execution. Despite the danger, many men and women from different countries volunteered for undercover work, driven by patriotism, ideology, or a sense of adventure.

Britain's MI6 and the Special Operations Executive (SOE)

In Britain, two major organizations handled much of the war's secret work:

1. **MI6 (Secret Intelligence Service)**: Focused on gathering intelligence outside the country. MI6 ran networks of agents across Europe and other regions. They aimed to learn about enemy troop movements, weapon production, and political plans.
2. **SOE (Special Operations Executive)**: Tasked with sabotage and supporting resistance movements in occupied countries. SOE dropped agents into France, Norway, Yugoslavia, and beyond. These agents supplied weapons, trained local fighters, and helped coordinate attacks on key German facilities.

Vera Atkins, a high-ranking female officer in SOE, oversaw many agents who parachuted into France. She was known for her strict standards and dedication, making sure her operatives were well-prepared. Sadly, some agents were caught by the Gestapo, facing torture or death. Yet their bravery slowed the German war machine and kept hope alive for occupied populations.

The Soviet NKVD and Smersh

In the Soviet Union, intelligence was handled by agencies such as the NKVD (later the KGB), along with a military counterintelligence unit named Smersh (an acronym roughly meaning "Death to Spies"). The Soviet secret services kept a tight watch on both their own citizens and enemies. They recruited agents to spy on German movements, sabotage supply lines, and pass information back to Moscow.

Soviet intelligence successes included the infiltration of German command structures, often carried out by partisans operating behind enemy lines. However, paranoia within the Soviet system meant even loyal agents were sometimes suspected of disloyalty. This environment made intelligence work extremely dangerous, yet the Soviets managed to gather vital information that helped them plan major operations like the counteroffensive at Stalingrad.

American Intelligence: The OSS

When the United States entered the war, it formed the Office of Strategic Services (OSS), an agency that would later become the CIA. Led by William "Wild Bill" Donovan, the OSS recruited a mix of academics, adventurers, and foreign language experts to run espionage missions in Europe and Asia.

The OSS operated behind enemy lines, parachuting agents into occupied France, Italy, and Burma. They helped organize local resistance groups, supplied them with weapons, and coordinated with Allied commands to sabotage rail lines, roads, and communication centers. These missions proved crucial in weakening Axis forces from within.

The German Abwehr and SD

Germany's main intelligence agency was the **Abwehr**, responsible for gathering information on enemy nations and sabotage operations. However, there was also the Sicherheitsdienst (SD), part of the SS, which often competed with the Abwehr. This rivalry led to internal confusion and mistrust, weakening Germany's overall intelligence efforts.

Though the Abwehr had some successes—recruiting spies in the Soviet Union and infiltrating resistance groups—it was often outmatched by the Allies' more coordinated systems. After some Abwehr officers tried to overthrow Hitler, the agency was essentially absorbed by the SD, but by then, it was too late to reverse the course of the war.

Codebreaking: The Battle of Wits

Beyond human spies, codebreaking was a vital part of the intelligence war. Cracking enemy codes allowed one side to read secret plans, while keeping their own codes safe prevented the enemy from doing the same.

1. **The Enigma Machine (Germany)**

    o   A key device Germany used to encrypt messages. It looked like a typewriter with rotating wheels (rotors). Every day, German operators set the machine to new configurations, believing it was unbreakable.
    o   British codebreakers at Bletchley Park, led by figures like **Alan Turing** and **Gordon Welchman**, developed techniques and early computers (called "bombes") to decipher many Enigma messages. This gave the Allies a huge advantage, especially against U-boats in the Atlantic.

2. **Purple Cipher (Japan)**

   o Japan's diplomatic code system was called "Purple." American codebreakers in the **Magic** program eventually broke this code, gaining insights into Japanese diplomatic traffic. Though not all military messages used Purple, the information gleaned helped shape Allied strategies.

3. **Soviet Codes**

   o The Soviets used one-time pads and other systems considered very secure. However, at times they also had lapses, allowing Germany to intercept some messages. Usually, the Soviets were highly secretive, so fully cracking their codes proved difficult.

4. **Naval Codes**

   o All major powers created separate codes for their navies. The outcome of many sea battles depended on codebreaking. The Allies often broke Japanese naval codes, leading to key victories like the Battle of Midway.
   o Germany's naval Enigma had extra security measures, but Allied codebreakers still found ways in, notably by capturing codebooks from U-boat weather ships or disabled submarines.

Secrets and Lies: Passing False Information

Part of intelligence work involved feeding the enemy with false information. This trick was best done through double agents, as we saw with **Agent Garbo** in Chapter 7. The success of Operation Fortitude (the D-Day deception) relied on codebreakers ensuring the

Germans believed the fake intelligence transmitted by these double agents.

To sell the lies, the Allies used captured German codes to hint to Berlin that the phony stories were correct. When Germany saw "confirmation" in their own code system, they trusted it. This elaborate cycle of sending and intercepting fake messages was one of the war's great mind games, saving countless Allied lives on D-Day.

Legendary Spies and Their Stories

- **Richard Sorge**: A Soviet spy who operated in Tokyo. He provided accurate intelligence about Japan's plans, allowing Stalin to shift divisions from Siberia to defend Moscow without worrying about a Japanese invasion. Eventually, Japan caught Sorge and executed him, but his information was vital.
- **Nancy Wake (The White Mouse)**: A New Zealand-born French Resistance agent. She helped Allied airmen escape occupied France and once killed an SS sentry with her bare hands. The Gestapo named her "The White Mouse" because she was so elusive.
- **Dušan Popov**: A Yugoslav double agent working for the British, known for his playboy lifestyle. He provided deceptive information to Germany while feeding real intelligence to the Allies. Some say he inspired the character James Bond.

These individuals show that spies came from many backgrounds. Some used charm and social connections to gather secrets, while others relied on stealth, sabotage, or high-level infiltration.

The Danger of Being Caught

Spies faced extreme risk. The Gestapo in Germany, the Kempeitai in Japan, and other secret police forces hunted them constantly. Agents had to worry about betrayals from colleagues, accidental slips, or simply being in the wrong place at the wrong time. Many were tortured for information, and entire networks collapsed if one agent broke under pressure.

In occupied countries, local people who helped spies also took huge risks. If discovered, entire families or villages could be punished. Yet despite the fear, many ordinary citizens cooperated, hiding agents in barns, attics, or cellars, providing false papers and guiding them through forests at night.

Code Talkers

Another fascinating piece of intelligence work in World War II involved **Native American code talkers**, especially from the Navajo tribe. The U.S. Marines recruited these men to send messages in their native language, which the Japanese never cracked. Navajo had no written form and was unknown outside the American Southwest, making it a perfect code base. Code talkers served in the Pacific, relaying vital orders quickly and securely.

Other Native American languages were also used in smaller roles, but the Navajo code talkers became famous for their speed and accuracy. Their service is a testament to how cultural diversity helped the Allied war effort.

Breaking the Japanese Diplomatic Code: Magic

American codebreakers formed the "Magic" team to work on Japanese ciphers, including the Purple cipher. They uncovered valuable diplomatic information, including Japan's negotiations with other Axis powers. While this did not always translate directly to military secrets, it offered a window into Japan's thinking. For instance, if a Japanese ambassador in Berlin sent a message about Germany's war plans, Magic might intercept it and inform U.S. commanders.

One key example was learning about Japan's stance before the attack on Pearl Harbor. Though the intelligence was not pieced together in time to prevent the attack fully, it showed cracks in U.S. intelligence processes—too many warnings came in, but nobody connected the dots.

Espionage in the Far East

In Asia, spies operated throughout China, Southeast Asia, and the Pacific islands. The Japanese had their own networks, but Allied agents often blended into local populations or worked with native guerrilla groups. The jungle environments made radio communication and resupply difficult, so agents had to rely on stealth and the good will of local villagers.

The OSS (American) and the British Special Operations Executive both sent teams into Burma and Malaya, where they trained rebels to ambush Japanese convoys, sabotage bridges, and gather intelligence. Conditions were brutal—tropical diseases, monsoons, and rough terrain tested every operative's endurance.

Post-War Revelations and Impact

After the war, many details about spies and codebreakers remained secret for decades. Slowly, the public learned how important the "invisible" side of the war had been:

- **Bletchley Park**: Britain finally acknowledged the role of codebreakers, crediting them with shortening the war by as much as two years.
- **Ultra**: The name given to intelligence gleaned from breaking German codes. Commanders like Eisenhower used Ultra to plan operations, but had to disguise the fact that they had such deep knowledge of enemy plans. This meant sometimes letting the Germans win small victories so they wouldn't suspect their codes were compromised.
- **Double-Cross System**: The Allies' management of double agents, which the public learned about much later. It showed how entire German spy rings in Britain were turned against the Nazis.

All this behind-the-scenes work shaped the outcome of many battles, saving countless lives. It also laid the groundwork for modern intelligence agencies.

Morality and Spycraft

Espionage raised moral questions. Spies had to lie and manipulate people. Codebreaking sometimes involved intercepting even personal messages. Some people questioned whether certain tactics violated international laws. Others argued that, in a total war scenario, there was no other choice if victory was to be achieved. Many of these debates continued after 1945, influencing how governments handled intelligence in peacetime.

Connecting Spies and Deception

Spies, lies, and codebreakers often worked hand in hand with the deception tactics from the previous chapter. A perfect example is how the Allies used Ultra intercepts to confirm whether the Germans believed their fake operations or not. If an intercepted message suggested doubt, they would amplify the deception. If the message showed that the Germans bought the story, they would maintain it.

This synergy proved to be a powerful weapon. It allowed the Allies to direct their forces more efficiently, while the Axis often moved units in response to false alarms. When combined with the raw power of the Allied industrial base, these intelligence and deception efforts made a major difference in how quickly the war ended.

CHAPTER 9

Unexpected Alliances and Strange Friendships

World War II was a conflict that drew nearly every corner of the globe into battle. With so many nations involved, alliances shifted and changed, sometimes in surprising ways. Countries that had once been enemies found themselves cooperating to fight a common foe, while others who seemed like natural allies turned against each other. In this chapter, we will explore these unexpected alliances and odd friendships, both at the national level and among individual people who found themselves on opposite sides.

The Complexity of Alliances

Before World War II officially began, a number of pacts and agreements set the stage for alliances that would later take shape:

- **Italy and Germany** signed the Pact of Steel in 1939, which pledged mutual support.
- **Japan** joined Germany and Italy in the Tripartite Pact, forming what became known as the Axis Powers.
- **Britain and France** declared war on Germany after the invasion of Poland, later joined by a broad group called the Allied Powers.

Yet these alliances were not as simple as one side against the other. Each country had its own goals, worries, and rivalries. As the war grew more intense, unexpected partnerships formed out of necessity.

The Soviet-German Non-Aggression Pact

One of the biggest surprises at the start of the war was the
Molotov-Ribbentrop Pact between the Soviet Union (led by Joseph
Stalin) and Nazi Germany (led by Adolf Hitler). Signed in August 1939,
it was a deal in which both sides promised not to attack each other.
Behind the scenes, they also agreed to divide parts of Eastern
Europe into "spheres of influence." Germany invaded Poland from
the west in September 1939, while the Soviet Union invaded it from
the east. This pact stunned the world because communism and
Nazism were considered extreme opposites.

Despite the agreement, neither Hitler nor Stalin truly trusted each
other. Many observers felt the pact was only a matter of
convenience. Indeed, by June 1941, Germany betrayed the pact with
Operation Barbarossa, the massive invasion of the Soviet Union.
This ended any hope of continued peace between the two powers
and turned the Soviets into an unexpected but vital ally of the
Western nations.

The Strange Alliance of the "Big Three"

After Germany attacked the Soviet Union in 1941, the Soviet Union
joined the Allies, forming an uneasy partnership with Britain and,
later, the United States. Winston Churchill (Britain), Franklin D.
Roosevelt (U.S.), and Joseph Stalin (Soviet Union) came to be known
as the "Big Three." This was surprising because Britain and the
United States distrusted Stalin's communist regime, and the Soviets
felt the same mistrust in return. However, the threat posed by Nazi
Germany forced them to work together.

For the rest of the war, these three leaders communicated through
letters, telegrams, and occasional face-to-face conferences (like the

Tehran Conference in 1943 and the Yalta Conference in 1945). Although they argued about strategies and post-war aims, they stayed united enough to defeat the Axis. Some found it odd to see Churchill, the staunch British conservative, sitting alongside Stalin, the communist dictator, and Roosevelt, the democratic president. Yet this surprising friendship led to major cooperative actions, such as Britain and the U.S. sending supplies to help the Soviets hold off Germany on the Eastern Front.

Italy's Shift in Alliances

Italy started the war on Germany's side under Benito Mussolini. However, by 1943, the war was going poorly for Italy, and Mussolini's government collapsed. A new Italian government under Marshal Pietro Badoglio eventually **signed an armistice** with the Allies in September 1943. This move shocked many Italians, as they had been told for years that Germany was their closest ally. Suddenly, German forces in Italy became enemies, and Italy itself became a battleground where Axis and Allied troops fought fiercely.

Some Italian soldiers joined the Allies, fighting against their former German partners. Others stayed loyal to Mussolini's puppet regime in northern Italy, supported by Germany. This split within Italy caused confusion, turmoil, and even family divisions. In a way, Italy's shift in alliances was one of the strangest turnarounds in the war, showing how quickly loyalties could change based on new realities.

Finland and the Soviets

Another unusual case was Finland. In 1939, the Soviet Union invaded Finland in what became known as the **Winter War**. Though Finland fought bravely, it eventually had to give up some territory. When Germany invaded the Soviet Union in 1941, Finland saw a chance to reclaim its lost lands. It joined forces with Germany, calling this conflict the **Continuation War**. Despite collaborating with Nazi Germany, Finland insisted it was only fighting to regain territory from the Soviets, not supporting Hitler's broader aims.

By 1944, as the tide of war turned against Germany, Finland negotiated an armistice with the Soviet Union and had to drive German troops out of Finnish territory. This series of changes, from being attacked by the Soviets to allying with Germany, then turning against Germany, makes Finland's situation one of the most complex alliances of the war.

Romania, Hungary, and Bulgaria

Other European countries, especially in Eastern Europe, found themselves shifting alliances under pressure.

- **Romania** initially allied with Germany to regain territory lost to the Soviet Union, sending troops to fight on the Eastern Front. But when the Soviets advanced into Romania in 1944, King Michael led a coup that deposed the pro-German government, and Romania switched sides to the Allies.
- **Hungary** was another German ally that tried to pull out of the war in 1944. Germany discovered these plans and occupied Hungary to keep it under Axis control, forcing the Hungarians to remain in the fight until Soviet troops overran the country.
- **Bulgaria** declared neutrality at first but later joined the Axis under pressure. Eventually, it left the Axis and declared war on Germany in 1944, after the Soviet Union threatened invasion.

These smaller nations faced huge dilemmas: remain loyal to Germany and risk being conquered by the Soviets, or switch sides and face retaliation from the Nazis. Many people in these countries experienced the war as a constant state of chaos, where friends and foes could swap places in a short time.

Vichy France and the Free French

When France fell to Germany in 1940, the northern part of the country was occupied by the Nazis, while the southern part became the **Vichy regime**, led by Marshal Philippe Pétain. This government officially cooperated with Germany, although many French citizens disliked it. Meanwhile, General Charles de Gaulle set up the **Free French** forces in Britain, vowing to continue fighting. This created a bizarre situation: two French authorities, each claiming legitimacy, but on opposite sides of the war.

As the war progressed, the Free French grew stronger, joining the Allies in North Africa and eventually in the liberation of France in

1944. The Vichy regime collapsed after the Allied landings in Normandy and the subsequent German defeat. Throughout the war, French families were divided between those supporting Vichy's collaboration with Germany and those backing De Gaulle's resistance. This was one of the war's saddest divisions, tearing apart communities and even families who had once stood side by side.

Surprising Friendships Among Soldiers

Beyond national alliances, there were stories of individual friendships that crossed enemy lines. In some areas, soldiers found brief common ground through small acts of humanity. For example:

1. **Truces to Gather Wounded**: On certain battlefields, opposing sides sometimes paused the fighting to collect their injured. Soldiers might share cigarettes or a quick chat before the truce ended.
2. **Christmas Gestures**: Though not as common as in World War I, there were still occasional holiday moments where soldiers on opposite sides sang carols or exchanged small gifts.
3. **Help from Civilians**: In occupied countries, a few kind civilians offered shelter to enemy soldiers, especially if they appeared wounded or lost. While rare, these actions show that not everyone viewed each other as lifelong enemies.

Such moments, while small, provided a glimpse of humanity in a brutal conflict. They remind us that war was fought by ordinary people who sometimes recognized each other's struggles, no matter which side they were on.

The Russo-Polish Tensions and Later Cooperation

Poland suffered greatly during the war, attacked by Germany from one side and the Soviet Union from the other. After being split and occupied, some Polish forces escaped to Britain and formed the

Polish Armed Forces in the West, including pilots who famously fought in the Battle of Britain. Meanwhile, within Poland, resistance groups fought against the Nazis, and Polish soldiers under Soviet command fought on the Eastern Front.

Relations between Poles and Soviets were tense, especially after events like the **Katyn Massacre** (where Soviet forces executed thousands of Polish officers). Still, in the face of the Nazi threat, some level of cooperation emerged on the battlefield, though it was uneasy. Polish troops fought bravely alongside the Red Army in pushing Germany back, hoping to liberate their homeland, but they also feared a new form of domination by the Soviet Union after the war.

Personal Bonds Among Leaders

While public alliances often drew attention, there were surprising personal friendships among leaders and generals:

- **Franklin D. Roosevelt (U.S.) and Winston Churchill (Britain)** had a close partnership, sending letters and meeting several times during the war. Their friendship helped coordinate strategies.
- **Winston Churchill and Joseph Stalin** shared a more strained relationship. However, during conferences, Churchill sometimes charmed Stalin with gifts or witty remarks. Stalin, in turn, would toast Churchill's leadership. Though they distrusted each other, they recognized the need to work together against Hitler.
- **Charles de Gaulle (Free French) and Roosevelt** had a frosty relationship. Roosevelt disliked De Gaulle's strong personality, and De Gaulle resented the United States for not fully recognizing his government at first. Despite these tensions, they allied for the sake of defeating Germany.

These relationships show that, even at the top levels, alliances were shaped by personal interactions as much as by national policy.

Neutral Countries with Hidden Links

Some nations managed to remain neutral or mostly out of the direct fighting. **Switzerland**, **Sweden**, **Spain**, and **Portugal** maintained official neutrality, but each had complex dealings with both the Allies and the Axis. For example:

- **Sweden** traded iron ore with Germany but also accepted Jewish refugees from neighboring countries.
- **Switzerland** was surrounded by Axis powers and had to tread carefully to avoid invasion. It kept strict border controls, but sometimes provided a safe haven for escapees.
- **Spain**, under Francisco Franco, did not join the war officially, but some Spanish volunteers (the Blue Division) went to fight alongside Germany on the Eastern Front.
- **Portugal**, under Salazar, allowed the Allies to use the Azores for naval and air bases, which helped with Atlantic patrols against U-boats.

These hidden links showed that neutrality could be more complicated than it seemed. Countries took part in limited partnerships, sometimes out of fear or economic necessity, while still trying to maintain a neutral stance.

Unexpected Turnarounds in the Pacific

In the Pacific theater, alliances were also fluid. **Thailand** initially joined with Japan, hoping to regain territory lost to neighbors. However, as Japan's fortunes fell, Thai leaders secretly contacted the Allies. Some Thai groups formed a resistance that worked with the Allied intelligence agencies. After the war, Thailand managed to avoid heavy punishment by arguing that the official declarations of war against the United States and Britain were invalid, as they had been forced by Japan.

In China, the situation was even more complex, with Chiang Kai-shek's Nationalist government receiving Allied support against Japan, while Mao Zedong's Communist forces also fought the Japanese but had an uneasy relationship with Chiang. Though they were both part of the Allied camp in name, Nationalists and Communists often clashed with each other. Still, at times, they cooperated to fight the common enemy of Japan.

The Human Side of Changing Alliances

Shifting alliances had a direct impact on ordinary people. Imagine a Romanian soldier fighting alongside the Germans on the Eastern Front, only to find that his country switched sides in 1944. Suddenly, the soldiers he used to call comrades become enemies, and the Allies he used to fight against become his new partners. This caused deep confusion and sometimes resentment.

Civilians in regions like the Balkans, Italy, or Eastern Europe might wake up one day to find themselves under the control of a new occupying army or a new government. Families were torn apart by political loyalties, and personal safety often depended on quickly adjusting to the changing power in charge.

Small Acts of Friendship Amid War

Despite the chaos, there were countless small acts of kindness that showed how human relationships could transcend politics. For instance:

- Prisoners of war sometimes received better treatment than official guidelines required, simply because guards felt sympathy or respect.
- Local villagers might share food with foreign soldiers passing through, even if they belonged to an occupying force, because they recognized the soldiers were hungry and far from home.
- Interpreters and liaison officers on both sides sometimes forged friendships that lasted for years, based on mutual admiration or shared interests (like music or sports).

These personal connections did not end the broader conflict, but they stand out as reminders that humanity can persist even amid global battles.

Lasting Impact on the War's Outcome

All these unexpected alliances and changed allegiances had major effects on World War II:

- The Soviet Union's alliance with Britain and the U.S. was critical in defeating Germany, as the Eastern Front tied down the majority of German troops.
- Italy's switch to the Allied side shortened the war in southern Europe and allowed the Allies to establish bases for bombing missions into Germany and the Balkans.
- Smaller countries' decisions—like Romania's or Bulgaria's—helped crumble the Axis coalition from within, hastening Nazi Germany's downfall.

At the same time, these alliances laid the groundwork for tensions that would arise after the war, especially between the Soviet Union and the Western Allies. But that is beyond our current focus, as we are staying within the World War II period.

CHAPTER 10

Weapons That Shocked the World

World War II was not only a clash of massive armies but also a race to develop the most advanced and devastating weapons. Each major power poured resources into creating tanks, planes, ships, and bombs that were bigger, faster, or more destructive than those of their enemies. Some of these weapons were tested on the battlefield with terrifying results, while others never moved beyond the prototype stage. In this chapter, we will look at the weapons that shocked the world—both the ones that saw heavy use and those that remained experimental curiosities.

The Rise of Modern Tanks

Tanks had been used in World War I, but they were still slow and unreliable. By World War II, tanks became a central part of armies. Different nations designed models with varying levels of armor, speed, and firepower.

Germany's Panzer Series

Early in the war, German Panzers (especially the Panzer III and IV) led blitzkrieg assaults, overpowering poorly equipped opponents. Later, Germany introduced heavier tanks like the **Tiger** and **Panther**. The Tiger had thick armor and a powerful 88mm gun that struck fear into Allied crews. However, it was expensive to produce and often broke down.

The **Panther** was considered by some as the best overall German tank of the war, with good armor and a high-velocity gun. Yet it, too, suffered from mechanical issues and required resources Germany could hardly spare.

Soviet T-34

The Soviet **T-34** is widely viewed as one of the best tanks of the war. It combined sloped armor for better protection, a reliable diesel engine, and a decent 76mm gun (later upgraded to 85mm). It was easier to produce in large numbers, which helped the Soviets overwhelm the German Panzers.

The T-34's simplicity made it a real game-changer, especially during the massive tank battles on the Eastern Front.

American M4 Sherman

The U.S. M4 Sherman was not as well-armed or armored as the German Tigers, but it was highly reliable and could be made in great quantities. The Allies used the Sherman in both Europe and the Pacific.

British variants like the Firefly added a more powerful gun to the Sherman chassis, allowing them to take on heavier German tanks.

British Churchill and Cromwell

Britain had several models, including the **Churchill**, which had thick armor and was great at supporting infantry but was slow. The **Cromwell** was faster, though lighter. British designers emphasized specialized tanks, creating "Hobart's Funnies" with mine flails, bridges, and flamethrowers for unusual battlefield tasks.

Naval Giants: Battleships and Carriers

Navies also raced to build bigger and more advanced warships. The role of aircraft carriers grew rapidly during the war, overshadowing even the mightiest battleships.

Yamato and Musashi (Japan)

The Japanese battleships **Yamato** and **Musashi** were the heaviest and most powerfully armed battleships ever built. They carried 18.1-inch guns that could out-range most Allied naval guns. However, their huge size made them prime targets for aircraft. Eventually, both were sunk by U.S. planes, showing that air power had become supreme at sea.

Bismarck and Tirpitz (Germany)

Germany built the battleships **Bismarck** and **Tirpitz**, hoping to challenge British naval supremacy. The Bismarck famously sank HMS Hood in 1941 but was hunted down by the British fleet soon after. The Tirpitz spent much of the war hiding in Norwegian fjords, posing a constant threat to Allied convoys but rarely engaging in open battle.

Both ships were eventually destroyed by air attacks, again demonstrating the rising dominance of aircraft in naval warfare.

Aircraft Carriers

The U.S. Navy put its faith in aircraft carriers like the **Enterprise**, **Yorktown**, and later the **Essex-class** carriers. Britain also had carriers, but the U.S. fielded them in greater numbers, especially in the Pacific.

Carrier battles, such as the **Battle of Midway**, changed the nature of naval warfare. Planes launched from carriers could strike enemy ships from hundreds of miles away, making big-gun battleships less relevant.

The Air War: Iconic Planes

World War II saw rapid advances in aircraft technology. Planes flew faster, carried heavier bomb loads, and introduced new combat tactics.

Fighter Aircraft

- **Supermarine Spitfire (Britain)**: Known for its role in the Battle of Britain, it had excellent maneuverability and speed.
- **Messerschmitt Bf 109 (Germany)**: A mainstay of the Luftwaffe's fighter force, used throughout the war.
- **Mitsubishi A6M "Zero" (Japan)**: Highly maneuverable Japanese fighter that dominated early in the war but lacked armor and self-sealing fuel tanks.
- **P-51 Mustang (U.S.)**: Gained fame escorting bombers over Germany with a long-range capability. Its arrival helped turn the tide in the air war over Europe.

Bombers

- **Heinkel He 111 and Ju 88 (Germany)**: German medium bombers used in the Blitz against Britain.
- **Avro Lancaster (Britain)**: A heavy bomber used for night raids over Germany, known for the famous "Dambusters" raid using bouncing bombs.
- **B-17 Flying Fortress and B-24 Liberator (U.S.)**: Long-range bombers that pounded German industry by day.
- **B-29 Superfortress (U.S.)**: An advanced bomber with pressurized cabins, used especially in the Pacific later in the war.

Jet and Rocket Aircraft

- **Messerschmitt Me 262 (Germany)**: The world's first operational jet fighter. Faster than Allied planes but introduced too late to change the war's outcome.
- **Heinkel He 162 and the "Komet" (Me 163)**: Other German jets or rocket-powered interceptors, often rushed into service with many technical issues.

The Fearsome V-Weapons

Germany developed a series of "V-weapons" (Vergeltungswaffen, meaning "vengeance weapons") in a desperate bid to turn the tide:

- **V-1 Flying Bomb ("Buzz Bomb")**: A pilotless, pulse-jet powered missile that flew at low altitude to strike British cities. Its distinctive buzzing sound terrified civilians.
- **V-2 Rocket**: The first ballistic missile in history. It traveled faster than sound, giving no warning before impact. Though terrifying, V-2 rockets required complex fuel and guidance systems, limiting their overall impact on the war.

- **V-3 "High Pressure Pump"**: A large gun intended to shell distant targets (like London) from the coast of France. It never became fully operational, though partial versions were tested.

These weapons caused fear and destruction but did not arrive in large enough numbers to change Germany's fate. They did, however, foreshadow the rocket age that would follow World War II.

Anti-Tank and Close-Support Weapons

Facing stronger and stronger tanks, all sides rushed to create better anti-tank weapons:

- **Bazooka (U.S.)**: A man-portable rocket launcher firing a shaped-charge warhead capable of penetrating tank armor.
- **Panzerschreck and Panzerfaust (Germany)**: Similar to the bazooka, used effectively against Allied tanks, especially in urban settings.
- **Anti-Tank Rifles and Guns**: Early in the war, some armies used oversized rifles to pierce light tanks, but as tank armor improved, these rifles became obsolete. Instead, heavier anti-tank guns (such as the German 88mm) dominated.

On the battlefield, these weapons gave infantry a chance to fight tanks, changing the balance and forcing tank crews to rely on infantry support to avoid ambush.

The Use of Flamethrowers and Incendiary Devices

Flamethrowers had existed since World War I, but in World War II they became more widespread for clearing bunkers or trenches:

- **Infantry Flamethrowers**: Carried on a soldier's back, spewing burning liquid at enemy fortifications. Extremely dangerous for both the operator (who risked being targeted) and the enemy.
- **Flamethrower Tanks**: Some tanks, such as the British Churchill Crocodile or the American Sherman "Zippo," replaced their main gun or a secondary weapon with a flamethrower. These were terrifying to defenders, especially in close-combat situations.

Additionally, both Axis and Allied forces used incendiary bombs during air raids, causing massive fires in cities like Dresden, Tokyo, Hamburg, and other locations. These firestorms created great destruction, showing that new weapons could be as horrifying as they were effective.

Artillery Innovations

Big guns still played a major role. World War II saw the use of heavy artillery, rocket launchers, and self-propelled guns:

- **Katyusha Rocket Launchers (Soviet)**: Mounted on trucks, these rocket launchers produced a chilling screech and delivered a barrage of explosives in seconds. They were simple, cheap, and highly mobile.
- **German Railway Guns**: Huge cannons like "Schwerer Gustav" and "Dora" fired massive shells over long distances, requiring special tracks and large crews. They were impressive but not always practical, as their movement was slow and they were easy to spot from the air.
- **Self-Propelled Artillery**: Tanks or tracked vehicles carrying large guns, such as the German StuG III or Soviet SU-76, helped provide direct fire support to advancing infantry and tanks.

Secret and Experimental Weapons

Many weapons never left the experimental stage but still capture our imagination:

- **The "Maus" Tank (Germany)**: A super-heavy tank project weighing over 180 tons. Only a couple of prototypes were made. It was impractical and consumed too much fuel.
- **Japanese Balloon Bombs**: Launched to ride high-altitude winds to North America. These bombs started a few small fires but did not have a major military impact.
- **Rocket-Powered Fighters (Me 163 Komet)**: Extremely fast but dangerous to pilots due to unstable rocket fuel and limited flight time.
- **British "Panjandrum"**: A giant, rocket-powered wheel of explosives intended to roll onto beaches during amphibious landings. Tests showed it was unstable and dangerous to its own side, so it was never used in battle.

While these odd inventions did not change the war, they demonstrate how far nations would go in search of an advantage.

The Atomic Bomb

Perhaps the most shocking weapon of World War II was the **atomic bomb**, developed by the United States under the Manhattan Project. This secret program brought together top scientists to build a device using nuclear fission. By mid-1945, the U.S. produced two bombs, **"Little Boy"** and **"Fat Man."**

- **Little Boy** was dropped on Hiroshima on August 6, 1945.
- **Fat Man** was dropped on Nagasaki on August 9, 1945.

The explosions were unlike anything the world had seen, causing immense destruction and loss of life. While some might argue the bombs hastened Japan's surrender, there is no doubt they introduced a terrifying new level of warfare. Even though we are not focusing on post-war events, it is clear that the atomic bomb changed the nature of conflict forever, at least during the final moments of WWII.

Weapons in the Pacific Theater

Apart from the atomic bomb, the Pacific war also saw unique weapons:

- **Amphibious Landing Craft**: The U.S. developed specialized boats (like the Higgins boat) for island invasions. They allowed troops to land directly on beaches under fire.
- **Kamikaze Planes**: As the war turned against Japan, some pilots carried out suicide attacks, diving their planes into Allied ships. This was a new and frightening tactic that, while destructive, could not ultimately stop the Allied advance.

These features, combined with fierce jungle fighting and naval battles, made the Pacific theater stand out from the European side of the war.

Psychological Impact

The appearance of new and terrifying weapons could shatter an enemy's morale. For instance, the Germans' early use of the Stuka dive-bomber created a distinctive siren wail that panicked troops below. The mere rumor of a Tiger tank in the area could make Allied units more cautious. Similarly, Allied bombers flying overhead made civilians in Axis cities dread nighttime raids.

Propaganda on all sides often exaggerated the power of these weapons. In some cases, that was enough to cause panic or force an enemy to overestimate the attacker's strength. But as the war wore on, experience taught many soldiers that even the most frightening weapon had vulnerabilities, especially if used poorly or in small numbers.

How Weapons Shaped Strategy

New weapons did not exist in a vacuum; they affected how generals planned campaigns:

- **Blitzkrieg** required fast tanks and close air support to break through enemy lines quickly.
- **Island Hopping** in the Pacific relied on carriers, amphibious craft, and air superiority to capture strategic islands.

- **Strategic Bombing** used large bomber fleets to target factories and supply routes, aiming to weaken the enemy's ability to fight.
- **Anti-Submarine Warfare** pitted destroyers, convoy tactics, and aircraft against German U-boats in the Battle of the Atlantic.

Each of these strategies revolved around certain key weapons. If one side gained a technological edge (like better radar, longer-range fighters, or more powerful tanks), it could shift the balance in major battles.

The Limits of Technology

Despite the impressive range of weapons, technology alone could not guarantee victory. Germany had advanced tanks and rocket weapons, but they lacked the industrial capacity to build them in sufficient numbers, and they fought on too many fronts at once. The Soviet Union and the United States, by contrast, leveraged mass production and simpler designs to overwhelm the Axis.

Similarly, Japan had skilled pilots and powerful battleships, but the U.S. outproduced them in ships, planes, and trained manpower. By 1944–1945, Japan simply could not replace lost carriers and veteran pilots, leading to desperate measures like kamikaze missions.

The Legacy of WWII Weapons

Though we are focusing on the wartime period, it is clear that the weapons of World War II left a huge mark on military thinking. They transformed land, sea, and air combat, showing that conflicts would increasingly rely on machines, advanced engineering, and science. Nations came to realize that the power of a well-equipped and well-supplied force could turn entire campaigns.

As we look back at the tanks, battleships, planes, rockets, and bombs that shook the world during WWII, we see human creativity at both its most impressive and its most destructive. These weapons were designed to end the war on the best terms for their makers, but they also brought about immense suffering. They stand as a reminder that technology in war can save lives by ending battles quickly—or can cost many lives if used relentlessly.

CHAPTER 11

The Wildest Characters of the War

World War II was not just about grand strategy or massive armies. It was also shaped by people—some brave, some ruthless, and many with larger-than-life personalities. This chapter focuses on some of the war's most colorful and unforgettable figures. They came from different countries, fought on different sides, and had very different goals. But all of them left behind stories that have stood out in history books, often because of their extreme, daring, or sometimes strange behavior.

Leaders with Big Personalities

1. Winston Churchill (Britain)

Winston Churchill, the British Prime Minister for much of the war, was known for his rousing speeches and bulldog spirit. He inspired the British people during the darkest days, such as the Blitz in 1940–1941. Beyond his politics, Churchill had many personal quirks:

- He loved cigars and could often be seen with one in his mouth.
- He enjoyed strong drinks, sometimes even sipping alcohol early in the day.
- Churchill was a gifted writer and painter, and he used these hobbies to relax during tense war moments.

He was also famous for his quick wit. When challenged or insulted, he could fire back with a sharp comeback. His leadership style combined seriousness, humor, and stubborn determination, shaping Britain's war effort and uniting the nation behind him.

2. Adolf Hitler (Germany)

Adolf Hitler, the dictator of Nazi Germany, was obviously one of the central figures of World War II. Although "wild" might not fully capture his infamous nature, there is no denying he was a forceful, dominating presence. Some of his traits and habits included:

- Long, dramatic speeches delivered with a fierce style that captivated many Germans at huge rallies.
- An extreme lifestyle that emphasized strict vegetarianism (later in life), non-smoking policies for those around him, and a deep interest in grand architecture.
- Intense paranoia about plots against him, which led to the creation of massive security systems and purges within his ranks.

He surrounded himself with loyal followers, but even they felt the weight of his unpredictable temper. Hitler's decisions often stemmed from his personal beliefs rather than sound military advice. This behavior became a major factor in Germany's eventual downfall.

3. Joseph Stalin (Soviet Union)

Joseph Stalin led the Soviet Union throughout the war after having already been in power for many years. He was known for his severe methods of control:

- Stalin ruled through fear, conducting purges of the Red Army's leadership just before the war, which weakened Soviet defenses.

- He had a habit of working late into the night, holding meetings until early morning.
- Suspicious by nature, Stalin trusted few people, even among his closest advisors.

Despite these traits, he became one of the "Big Three" Allied leaders, along with Churchill and Roosevelt. Many Soviet citizens saw him as a hero who led them to victory over Nazi Germany, but millions also suffered under his harsh regime.

4. Benito Mussolini (Italy)

Benito Mussolini was Italy's fascist dictator, who dreamed of reviving the glory of the old Roman Empire. Known for his bombastic speeches and dramatic gestures:

- He stood on balconies, gesturing with forceful arm movements as he addressed the crowds.
- Mussolini had a high opinion of himself, calling himself "Il Duce" (The Leader).
- In private, he could be moody, and his leadership style often changed based on his personal feelings rather than logic.

His wild ambition led Italy into disastrous campaigns in Greece and North Africa. Eventually, his own people turned against him, and he lost power in 1943.

Military Commanders with Flamboyant Traits

1. General Douglas MacArthur (United States)

General Douglas MacArthur was a key figure in the Pacific theater:

- Known for his corncob pipe and his trademark sunglasses, he cut a striking figure.
- MacArthur famously left the Philippines in 1942, saying, "I shall return," which became a promise he later fulfilled by liberating the islands from Japanese occupation.
- He had a strong ego and often clashed with other military leaders. Yet, many of his troops were fiercely loyal to him, respecting his bold vision and confidence.

2. General George S. Patton (United States)

General George Patton was another American commander known for his fiery personality and strict discipline:

- He carried ivory-handled pistols on his belt, a sign of his flashy style.
- Patton believed in aggressive warfare and constantly pushed his troops to move fast and strike hard.
- Sometimes his temper got him into trouble, such as when he slapped two soldiers who were suffering from combat stress, causing a scandal.

Despite these controversies, Patton's rapid advances through Europe in 1944–1945 contributed greatly to the Allied victory.

3. Field Marshal Bernard Montgomery (Britain)

Often called "Monty," Field Marshal Bernard Montgomery was a British commander who led forces in North Africa and later in the Normandy campaign:

- Known for his trademark beret and plain-spoken manner.
- He insisted on thorough planning and had a strong belief in doing things his way.
- Montgomery and Patton disliked each other, competing for fame and credit in the campaigns against Germany.

Montgomery's careful leadership helped win the important Battle of El Alamein in North Africa, boosting Allied morale at a critical time.

4. Field Marshal Erwin Rommel (Germany)

Nicknamed the "Desert Fox," Erwin Rommel became famous during the North African campaign:

- He was admired by both German and Allied troops for his chivalry and fair treatment of prisoners.
- Rommel's daring maneuvers and swift attacks in the desert earned him respect, though his resources were often limited.
- Later involved (indirectly) in a plot to remove Hitler, he faced suspicion and was forced to end his own life.

Rommel stood out as one of the war's most brilliant tank commanders, leaving a legacy as an honorable opponent despite serving under the Nazi regime.

Heroes from the Ranks

Not all wild characters were generals. Many lesser-known soldiers performed remarkable feats or showed unique personalities that left strong impressions.

1. Audie Murphy (United States)

Audie Murphy was one of the most decorated American soldiers of the war. He started as a poor Texas farm boy but quickly showed bravery under fire:

- At 19, he received the Medal of Honor after holding off an entire German company by himself for nearly an hour.
- He climbed onto a burning tank destroyer to use its machine gun, despite being wounded in the leg.

- After the war, he became a Hollywood actor, starring in movies and even playing himself in a film about his life.

2. Nancy Wake (New Zealand / France)

Nancy Wake, also known as the "White Mouse," was a courageous secret agent who worked with the French Resistance:

- She helped Allied airmen escape occupied France and organized sabotage missions.
- The Gestapo placed a large bounty on her head, calling her the "White Mouse" because she was so elusive.
- Known for her wit and bravery, she once killed an SS guard with her bare hands during a mission.

Her daring exploits made her one of the war's most famous female spies and earned her high decorations from multiple Allied nations.

3. Otto Skorzeny (Germany)

Otto Skorzeny was a German commando officer who gained fame for rescuing Italian leader Benito Mussolini from captivity in 1943:

- His bold glider-borne assault on the mountain hotel where Mussolini was held became legendary.
- Skorzeny led other special operations, sometimes wearing enemy uniforms to cause confusion.
- After the war, he was tried but later escaped serious punishment, partly due to the nature of his missions and the confusion around special operations laws.

He became a symbol of Nazi Germany's commando capability, admired by some for his daring, yet still tied to a brutal regime.

Civilians Who Stood Out

1. Oskar Schindler (Germany)

Though Schindler started as a war profiteer and member of the Nazi Party, he ended up saving over a thousand Jewish lives:

- He ran a factory using Jewish labor but soon realized the horrors they faced.
- By bribing officials and forging paperwork, Schindler turned his factory into a safe haven, preventing them from being sent to death camps.
- After the war, he was penniless, but many of those he saved honored him for his bravery and humanity.

His story shows that, even under a harsh regime, some people did extraordinary things to protect others.

2. Irena Sendler (Poland)

Irena Sendler was a Polish social worker who helped smuggle around 2,500 Jewish children out of the Warsaw Ghetto:

- She forged documents and worked with a network of helpers to shelter these children, often placing them in Catholic convents or with Polish families.
- The Gestapo arrested her, but Sendler never revealed the children's locations.
- She survived torture and continued her humanitarian work after the war.

Her efforts went unrecognized for many years, but she is now celebrated as one of the war's quiet heroes.

Wild Stories and Legends

World War II gave rise to many legends about people who performed unbelievable feats or had strange habits. Some may be exaggerated, but they reveal how stories spread during times of conflict:

- **The Ghost Sniper**: In Stalingrad, Soviet snipers gained a mythical reputation. Men like Vasily Zaytsev became folk heroes. Some German soldiers believed a single sniper might be taking impossible shots from hidden positions.
- **Churchill's Daring Escape**: Before WWII, during the Boer War (around 1900), Winston Churchill escaped from a prison camp in South Africa, boosting his earlier heroic image. Though this was not part of WWII, it added to Churchill's legend during the later conflict.
- **The Soldier Who Wouldn't Quit**: Stories of Japanese holdouts who kept fighting or hiding in jungles for years after 1945 point to the extreme dedication (or confusion) of some individuals. Though these events happened after WWII officially ended, they stem from the same era's mindset.

Strange Habits and Superstitions

Many of these characters had odd routines or superstitions:

- **Hitler's Astrologers**: Some historians note that Hitler consulted people who claimed to predict the future, especially when he was desperate.
- **Stalin's Late-Night Gatherings**: Stalin often invited his closest allies to all-night dinners, expecting them to stay until he decided to sleep.
- **MacArthur's Sunglasses**: He rarely appeared in public without them, almost as if they were a lucky charm.

- **Patton's Belief in Reincarnation**: Patton famously said he believed he had been a warrior in past lives, such as during ancient Roman times. This belief influenced his bold leadership style.

These habits might seem silly or strange today, but they played a part in shaping how these figures acted under pressure.

The Power of Personality in War

Why do these wild characters matter? In a conflict as huge as World War II, the actions of individuals could influence entire armies or nations. Leaders with strong personal styles could inspire troops to fight harder—or cause disastrous mistakes through stubbornness. Secret agents who were fearless or unpredictable could outsmart enemy defenses. Even civilians with unusual courage saved thousands of lives.

Many soldiers followed their leaders with almost religious devotion. People like Hitler, Stalin, or Mussolini built cults of personality, using propaganda to appear larger than life. Others, like Churchill or Roosevelt, united nations through words of hope and determination rather than fear. In the heat of battle, having a leader who radiated confidence could make the difference between holding a line and breaking into a retreat.

Criticisms and Controversies

Not all these figures are admired. Some have dark legacies due to their brutality or flawed decisions:

- Hitler started the war in Europe, committed mass atrocities, and led Germany to ruin.
- Stalin's leadership helped defeat Nazism, but he also caused millions of deaths through purges and forced policies.
- Mussolini's dream of empire led Italy into a disastrous war it was not ready for.
- Even Allied commanders like Patton or Montgomery have critics who say they chased personal glory, risking soldier's lives.

At the same time, the war also produced heroes who remain widely respected. People like Oskar Schindler, Irena Sendler, Audie Murphy, and Nancy Wake are remembered for their courage and selflessness in terrible times.

Lessons Learned

From these wild characters, we learn that war is not just fought by faceless armies. Individual personalities can shape strategy, morale, and even the outcome of key battles. Some used their charisma to rally nations, while others used fear. Some saw war as a stage to prove their bravery or cunning, and others simply wanted to help the helpless. Their stories remind us that humans can be both destructive and compassionate under extreme conditions.

As we move on to the next chapter, we'll dive into stories of **Daring Naval Adventures and Submarine Tales**. Just as the war on land had fearless characters, the war at sea had its share of bold captains, cunning submarine crews, and heroic rescue missions. These maritime events added another layer of drama to an already global conflict.

CHAPTER 12

Daring Naval Adventures and Submarine Tales

World War II was fought across the globe's oceans as well as on land. Navies battled for control of vital sea lanes, protecting or disrupting the flow of troops and supplies. Submarines prowled beneath the waves, launching surprise attacks. Aircraft carriers, battleships, cruisers, and destroyers played crucial roles in campaigns that spanned from the Atlantic to the Pacific. In this chapter, we look at some of the most daring naval adventures and remarkable submarine stories that shaped the war at sea.

The Battle of the Atlantic

One of the longest and most critical campaigns was the **Battle of the Atlantic**, where German U-boats tried to cut off Britain's supply lines. Allied convoys, carrying food, weapons, and fuel, were escorted by warships and aircraft, facing a hidden threat beneath the waves.

- **Wolf Packs**: German U-boat commander Karl Dönitz developed the "wolf pack" tactic, where multiple submarines would converge on a convoy at night, attacking from different angles.
- **Technology Race**: Allies responded with better sonar (called ASDIC), radar, and the breaking of German naval codes (Enigma), allowing them to direct escorts more effectively.
- **Escorts and Air Cover**: Destroyers, corvettes, and later escort carriers fought off U-boats. Long-range patrol aircraft from Greenland or Iceland also helped cover the "mid-Atlantic gap," an area previously out of reach for most planes.

This back-and-forth struggle decided whether Britain could remain in the war. Had the U-boats succeeded in starving Britain of supplies, the entire conflict might have ended differently.

Hunting the Bismarck

The German battleship **Bismarck** was a major threat to Allied shipping. In May 1941, it sunk the British battlecruiser **HMS Hood**, one of the Royal Navy's most famous ships, in a brief but devastating engagement. Shocked by this loss, the British launched a massive hunt to track down and destroy the Bismarck before it could return to safety.

- **Spotting the Bismarck**: British reconnaissance planes scoured the Atlantic, eventually finding the battleship.
- **Final Showdown**: British ships, including the battleship King George V and the cruiser HMS Dorsetshire, engaged the Bismarck, hammering it with shells and torpedoes.
- **Sinking**: The Bismarck was scuttled by its crew after suffering heavy damage, though debate remains about whether British torpedoes delivered the final blow.

This dramatic chase demonstrated the Royal Navy's determination and the vulnerability of even the largest battleships when targeted by a full fleet.

The Doolittle Raid

While primarily an air strike, the Doolittle Raid in April 1942 was a naval adventure as well. The U.S. Navy used the carrier **USS Hornet** to launch 16 B-25 Mitchell bombers against Tokyo, Japan. This was the first time medium bombers had taken off from a carrier, an unusual feat:

- **Bold Planning**: Led by Lieutenant Colonel James Doolittle, the mission aimed to show Japan that the U.S. could strike the Japanese home islands.
- **Early Launch**: The task force was spotted by a Japanese patrol boat, forcing an earlier-than-planned takeoff.
- **Limited Damage, Huge Morale Boost**: Though the physical damage to Tokyo was small, the raid shocked Japan and greatly boosted American morale after the attack on Pearl Harbor.

Most planes ran out of fuel and crash-landed in China. Some crew members were captured by Japanese forces, facing harsh conditions. Nevertheless, the raid's daring spirit became legendary.

"Midget Submarines" at Pearl Harbor

The surprise attack on **Pearl Harbor** on December 7, 1941, is well known for Japan's aerial strike. But Japan also deployed five small "midget submarines" to penetrate the harbor:

- **Two-Man Crews**: Each mini-sub had just two sailors, packed into a tight, cramped space.
- **Limited Success**: Most were sunk or captured. One might have fired torpedoes, but it did not change the battle's outcome.
- **Aftermath**: This attempt showed Japan's willingness to use unconventional methods, although the main blow at Pearl Harbor still came from carrier-based aircraft.

Despite failing, these mini-subs reflect the inventive naval tactics used throughout the war.

U-Boat Aces and Notable Captains

German U-boat commanders, sometimes called "aces," led crews that sank many Allied ships. Figures like **Otto Kretschmer** and **Wolfgang Lüth** gained fame for their high "tonnage" (the total weight of ships they destroyed). Yet life on a U-boat was tough:

- **Cramped Conditions**: Submariners lived among torpedoes, machinery, and limited supplies.
- **Dangerous Missions**: A single depth charge from an escort ship could crack the hull, dooming the entire submarine.
- **Morale and Camaraderie**: Crews formed tight bonds, relying on each other in the darkness beneath the ocean's surface.

On the Allied side, captains like **Frederick John Walker** (Royal Navy) developed new anti-submarine tactics, forming special groups of ships dedicated to hunting U-boats. These groups helped turn the tide by mid-1943, when Allied escorts finally gained the upper hand.

The Tragedy of Convoys and Civilian Ships

Not all daring naval tales involve warships. Merchant sailors and civilian mariners also faced danger. Convoys braved enemy submarines, storms, and long voyages to deliver essential cargo. Sometimes:

- Ships caught fire when torpedoed, forcing desperate evacuations in lifeboats.
- Survivors drifted for days in open rafts, hoping to be spotted by a friendly vessel or a patrol plane.
- Hospital ships, marked with large red crosses, were supposed to be off-limits, but some were still attacked by mistake or in violation of international rules.

These stories remind us that the war at sea was not just battleships and submarines; it also involved thousands of everyday seamen doing their jobs under deadly threat.

The Pacific War at Sea

Across the vast Pacific, the U.S. Navy and the Imperial Japanese Navy clashed in major carrier battles. These encounters showed how aircraft carriers had become the key to naval power.

1. **Battle of the Coral Sea (May 1942)**

   - The first naval battle in history where opposing ships never saw or fired directly at each other. All attacks were carried out by carrier-based aircraft.
   - Though considered a tactical victory for Japan (they sank more ships), it was a strategic win for the Allies because it stopped Japan's advance toward Australia.

2. **Battle of Midway (June 1942)**

    ○ Often seen as the turning point in the Pacific War.
    ○ The U.S. Navy, helped by codebreakers, ambushed the Japanese fleet, sinking four Japanese carriers at the cost of one American carrier (USS Yorktown).
    ○ This major blow crippled Japan's ability to conduct large-scale carrier operations.

3. **Battles Around Guadalcanal (1942–1943)**

    ○ Fierce nighttime naval fights between American and Japanese ships in what came to be called "Ironbottom Sound" (so many ships were sunk there).
    ○ Both sides lost cruisers, destroyers, and carriers, but eventually, the U.S. Navy gained the upper hand, securing supply lines to American ground forces on the island.

Kamikaze Attacks

As Japan's situation became desperate, the Imperial Japanese Navy and Air Force began using **kamikaze** tactics:

- **Suicide Missions**: Pilots intentionally crashed planes into Allied ships, carrying bombs or explosives.
- **Effects on Morale**: Allied sailors were horrified by the prospect of incoming pilots with no regard for their own lives. Heavy losses occurred on ships near the Japanese homeland.
- **Limitations**: While terrifying and sometimes effective, kamikaze attacks could not stop the overwhelming Allied naval power, especially as the war progressed into 1945.

These attacks highlight the extreme measures some nations took in a war that felt like it might drag on indefinitely.

Special Operations at Sea

Naval battles were not limited to giant ships. Smaller, specialized forces also carried out daring missions:

1. **Italian Human Torpedoes**
   - The Decima Flottiglia MAS used "human torpedoes" and "frogmen" to sneak into Allied harbors and attach explosives to enemy ships.
   - They damaged or sank several British ships in the Mediterranean, showing how a few brave men could strike powerful fleets.
2. **British Midget Submarines (X-Craft)**
   - The Royal Navy used mini-subs to attack German battleships like the Tirpitz, hidden in Norwegian fjords.
   - Commandos placed explosive charges beneath the ship's hull, damaging it and limiting its effectiveness.

These operations required intense training and nerves of steel, as failure often meant death or capture.

Submarines in the Pacific

While German U-boats grabbed headlines in the Atlantic, the U.S. submarine force waged a powerful campaign against Japanese shipping in the Pacific. Over time, American subs cut off essential supplies of food and raw materials to the Japanese home islands:

- **Limited Early Success**: Faulty torpedoes plagued U.S. subs in 1942–1943. Known as the "Mark 14 torpedo problem," many would fail to explode or run off course.
- **Improved Reliability**: Once fixes were made, submarine captains scored huge victories, sinking numerous cargo ships and warships.
- **Strategic Impact**: By 1945, Japan's economy was choking, as submarines had sunk so many merchant vessels that the country faced shortages of oil, rubber, and metals.

In the Pacific, submarines were a key factor in paralyzing Japan's ability to keep fighting.

Heroic Rescues and Survival Tales

The war at sea also produced heart-pounding stories of rescue:

- **USS Tang Rescue**: When the American submarine USS Tang sank after being hit by its own torpedo (a tragic accident), some crew members managed to escape from the sub's forward compartments using an emergency escape device.
- **Downed Airmen**: U.S. Navy "Dumbo" missions involved flying patrol aircraft looking for airmen who had ditched in the ocean. These aircraft, if fitted with pontoons, could land to pick up survivors.
- **Lifeboat Odysseys**: Civilians and sailors from torpedoed ships sometimes drifted for weeks, surviving on limited rations and rainwater, until they reached land or were spotted by rescue vessels.

Such stories highlight the will to survive against overwhelming odds in the lonely expanses of the sea.

Coastal Defenses and Small Craft

Not all naval action took place on the high seas. Coastlines turned into battle zones as well:

- **Amphibious Assaults**: From Normandy to Iwo Jima, landing craft delivered troops onto beaches under fire. Ships shelled enemy positions onshore to give cover.
- **PT Boats**: In the Pacific, the U.S. used small, fast "Patrol Torpedo" boats (PT boats) for hit-and-run attacks. John F. Kennedy, who later became a U.S. President, commanded PT-109, which was rammed and sunk by a Japanese destroyer. His leadership in saving his crew became legendary.
- **Soviet River Flotillas**: On the Eastern Front, the Soviets used gunboats and small craft to patrol major rivers and lakes, supporting ground troops in amphibious operations.

These smaller-scale naval engagements were just as dangerous as big battles, often fought in tight waters and at close range.

Lessons from the War at Sea

1. **Air Power at Sea**: Aircraft carriers replaced battleships as the primary tools for naval dominance.
2. **Submarine Warfare**: Submarines could devastate merchant shipping, influencing whether entire nations starved or survived.
3. **Convoy Systems**: Coordinated convoy escorts showed that teamwork and technology (radar, sonar, codebreaking) could defeat submarine threats.

4. **Innovation and Risks**: Human torpedoes, mini-subs, and kamikazes illustrated the creative and desperate lengths nations would go to gain an edge.

The Enduring Fascination with Naval Adventures

Even decades later, people remain fascinated by these naval and submarine stories. Wrecks of famous ships—like the Bismarck, found under the ocean—tell silent tales of epic struggles. Submarine museums around the world show how men lived and fought in cramped steel tubes beneath the sea. Survivors' accounts of storms, battles, and rescues remind us of the raw courage it took to face the unknown ocean.

Naval warfare in World War II stands out because of the dramatic shift from big guns to carrier aviation. Submarine campaigns also changed how wars were fought, giving smaller craft the power to challenge entire fleets or cripple a nation's trade. Above all, these stories highlight the bravery and resourcefulness of sailors, submariners, and pilots who risked their lives on the world's oceans.

CHAPTER 13

Miraculous Survival Stories

World War II was a time of immense destruction, with entire cities reduced to rubble, vast armies clashing across continents, and naval battles raging at sea. Amid all this tragedy and turmoil, there were also stories that seemed nearly impossible—accounts of people who survived situations so dire that onlookers called them miracles. These tales of survival came from every theater of the war, whether in bombed-out city streets, remote jungles, frozen tundra, or the open ocean. Some of these stories involved a stroke of luck, while others showed how courage and resourcefulness could keep someone alive against all odds.

Living Through Relentless Bombings

During the Blitz in Britain, especially in places like London, Coventry, and other major cities, constant air raids forced civilians to seek shelter night after night. Families crouched in underground stations, makeshift backyard shelters, or the basements of large buildings. Many houses suffered direct hits, leaving some residents trapped beneath their own floors or pinned by collapsed beams. Time and again, rescue crews discovered survivors who had been buried for hours or even days. A person might owe their life to a sturdy kitchen table that withstood the falling ceiling, or to the way the rubble formed a small protective pocket. Although these circumstances seemed random, those who endured such brushes with death often spoke of feeling calm or determined as they waited to be rescued.

In the German cities that later faced heavy bombing, similar stories emerged. The city of Hamburg experienced a devastating firestorm in 1943, where superheated winds made streets glow with heat. Yet a few people escaped through sheer quick thinking, such as finding shelter in a concrete bunker at the last second or diving into a canal to avoid the flames rushing through the streets. These survivors sometimes lost everything they owned, but they held onto life despite the extreme conditions. In interviews after the war, many described thinking each moment would be their last, only to discover a path to safety. Those who came out of the firestorm areas reported seeing entire neighborhoods turned to ash, with only a handful of buildings standing. Their survival felt like a gift that could never be fully explained.

Surviving the Siege and the Cold

On the Eastern Front, the war involved not only bombs and bullets but also the brutal force of weather. Cities like Leningrad, which endured a siege of nearly nine hundred days, became places of extraordinary endurance. Citizens lived for months without reliable heat, electricity, or sufficient food. In the worst periods of winter, temperatures dropped well below freezing, and people had to burn furniture, books, and any scrap of wood they could find to stay warm. Countless died of starvation, yet stories also spread of families who managed to survive by sharing the smallest rations or by growing vegetables in indoor pots. Some recounted how they found hidden stores of flour or made soup from leather scraps. These tales underscored the powerful will to live, even when a city was surrounded by enemy lines.

In Stalingrad, soldiers and civilians alike faced daily threats from snipers, artillery shells, and freezing weather. Many fought for survival in the ruins of buildings, constructing makeshift bunkers out of collapsed walls and rubble. They had to melt snow for drinking water and scrounge for any form of nourishment. Occasionally, a Soviet or German soldier found himself cut off from his unit. Hiding in basements, he might share a moment of desperate humanity with an enemy soldier who was equally lost. Although such stories were rare, they showed that, at times, enemies became reluctant companions in the face of harsh conditions. Those who lived through Stalingrad often recalled intense hunger and constant danger, yet also moments of surprising fortune, such as discovering an untouched store of supplies or being overlooked by an enemy patrol.

Downed Pilots Who Found a Way

Air combat during the war resulted in many pilots and aircrew being shot down over hostile territory. Surviving a crash was often just the beginning. Some managed to parachute out of flaming bombers, landing miles behind enemy lines. They might have broken bones or burns, yet they knew that capture or death was nearly certain unless they could hide or escape. Resistance networks in Occupied Europe often took these pilots in, moving them from safe house to safe house, forging documents, and guiding them toward neutral countries like Spain or Switzerland. A British pilot might stay in a barn on a French farm, covered with straw to avoid detection, while local villagers brought small bits of bread and water. When the time was right, a guide would lead him on foot across border checkpoints, avoiding patrols. Many who survived such journeys described them as a mixture of terror and gratitude. A single knock on the door could mean discovery, yet the unwavering kindness of strangers kept them going.

In the Pacific, downed airmen sometimes drifted at sea in inflatable rafts. They battled scorching sun, saltwater sores, and sharks circling nearby. A few managed to survive for weeks by catching rain in fabric sheets, spearing fish with makeshift tools, and hoping that Allied search planes would spot them. When rescue finally arrived, they were often delirious, sunburned, and near starvation. Some of these pilots returned to active duty after recovering, determined to keep fighting. Their stories spread across air bases, giving hope to others who feared ditching into the ocean. In some cases, entire crews survived plane crashes on remote islands. Local islanders might help them, or they might have to build temporary shelters until a submarine or seaplane could be summoned for rescue.

Enduring the Jungle's Unknowns

The war in Southeast Asia and the Pacific islands introduced countless soldiers to harsh tropical conditions. Those who became separated from their units faced hazards like venomous snakes, tropical diseases, and thick jungle canopies that made navigation nearly impossible. A small group of Allied troops might find themselves miles behind Japanese lines, forced to move silently to avoid detection. They learned to collect drinkable water from large leaves, craft basic snares for small animals, and find edible plants by observing local people or by trial and error. Malaria and dysentery took a heavy toll, but a few defied the odds by carefully rationing whatever medical supplies they carried. Sometimes they were helped by friendly villagers who despised the occupying forces. For instance, a group of American airmen in Burma once walked more than a hundred miles to reach safety, guided by a local hunter who showed them a hidden track through the dense forest. That journey took them several weeks, during which they survived mostly on wild fruits and small game. When they finally reached an Allied outpost, they were so emaciated that comrades struggled to recognize them.

Facing the Desert Sun

In North Africa, the battlefields were scorching in daytime and chilling at night. Vehicle breakdowns and disrupted supply lines meant that soldiers could be stranded far from help. Both Axis and Allied troops sometimes found themselves low on water, wandering in search of wells or an oasis. Stories emerged of men who traveled on foot for days, using the stars to guide them, until they stumbled upon a friendly encampment. They might arrive half-crazed from heat exhaustion. On more than one occasion, soldiers from opposing sides made an unspoken truce around a water source, sharing the little they had. While such events were rare, they illustrated how essential water was in the desert. A single canteen could mean the difference between life and death. Some survivors managed to remain alive by drawing on training in desert survival, such as traveling at night, staying in the shade whenever possible, and conserving sweat rather than gulping water. Their endurance became legendary in their units, and newcomers soon learned the importance of desert discipline.

Overcoming Fear Beneath the Waves

Survival stories at sea were some of the most dramatic. Merchant ships crossing the Atlantic faced German U-boat attacks, often in the dead of night. A single torpedo could break a vessel in two, leaving the crew to flounder in rough waters. Those who made it onto rafts or lifeboats had to endure cold, hunger, and sometimes storms. Rescues might come hours later or might never come at all. Some men floated for weeks, living on rainwater and sharing meager rations. A few times, a U-boat captain surfaced near survivors and gave them basic directions or supplies before disappearing again. Although these gestures of mercy were not the norm, they did happen, and survivors passed along these stories. When rescue ships appeared on the horizon, the men in the lifeboats often used mirrors, flares, or shouted at the top of their lungs to attract attention. In the Pacific, survivors had to watch out for sharks and strong currents that could pull them farther from safe routes. Overcoming the psychological strain was just as hard as surviving physically. Many sang songs or recited prayers to keep their spirits up.

Instances of Strange Good Fortune

Amid the many accounts of perseverance and courage, there were also tales of bizarre luck. A bomb might pierce a roof and land in a kitchen but fail to detonate, leaving the occupants unharmed. A fighter plane might crash-land, yet the pilot walked away with barely a scratch. A soldier trapped under rubble might find an airway that kept him breathing until rescuers arrived days later. People who experienced these strange strokes of fortune often said they felt an unexplained calm or a sense that they were meant to survive. Sometimes entire families emerged from collapsed houses, shaking dust off their clothes, while neighbors on both sides had no such luck. Many struggled with guilt afterward, wondering why they survived when so many did not. Others took it as a sign to live their remaining life to the fullest, determined to rebuild once the war ended.

Tales of Altruism and Sacrifice

Some survival stories also highlight how people saved others through selfless acts. During heavy bombing raids, neighbors rushed into burning buildings to help those trapped inside, even when it meant risking their own lives. In besieged cities, individuals shared the last of their food or carried the injured through dangerous streets. Soldiers sometimes dragged wounded comrades across rivers under enemy fire. Even in prisoner-of-war situations, as we will see in the next chapter, certain individuals risked punishment or death to help fellow inmates survive. These accounts remind us that even in the darkest hours, empathy and kindness could shine through.

On the Eastern Front, where the fighting was especially intense, there are records of local villagers providing bread or soup to soldiers of both sides, simply because they saw men in need. Such compassion could backfire if occupying forces discovered it, leading to harsh reprisals. Nonetheless, these brave villagers felt they had a moral duty to aid anyone who was hungry or injured. Some did so secretly at night, leaving food parcels by the roadside. Soldiers who benefited from these gestures might never learn the identities of their benefactors, but they carried the memory of that small spark of humanity in the midst of overwhelming violence.

Medical Miracles in the Field

In the midst of battle, field surgeons and medical staff had to perform complex operations using only the supplies on hand. Many wounded soldiers survived injuries that might have been fatal in earlier wars, thanks to advances in antibiotics like penicillin and improved surgical techniques. There were cases of men losing limbs to mines or artillery shells yet receiving swift medical care that prevented infection. Some recovered well enough to return home or even rejoin their units. Nurses, often working under fire, showed remarkable calm, transfusing blood, setting broken bones, and comforting the dying. Tales of medics crossing minefields to reach the wounded or operating in a tent surrounded by explosions became part of the war's lore. The fact that any soldier pulled through such circumstances was viewed as little short of miraculous, testifying to the skill and tenacity of those providing care.

Psychological Strength and the Will to Live

Survival is not just physical; it involves mental and emotional resilience as well. Many survivors described a fierce inner conviction that they must not die. This conviction drove them to crawl through rubble, limp through enemy territory, or cling to a raft despite hunger and thirst. In diaries written during sieges or captivity, one finds repeated references to hope. Soldiers and civilians alike clung to the thought of seeing loved ones again. Those who had religious faith might have prayed ceaselessly. Others held onto a photograph, a letter, or a simple keepsake that reminded them of home. The mind's ability to sustain a will to live was often praised as the key factor that made the difference between death and survival.

Some individuals who endured near-death experiences wrote about vivid impressions that stayed with them forever. A British seaman once described how, after his ship sank, he floated alone in the Atlantic with only a small piece of wreckage. He recalled being overtaken by a strange calm, telling himself that he was going to see the sun rise again. Hours later, he was rescued by a passing ship. When he told his story, he said that the image of that sunrise was the most beautiful sight he ever witnessed. Another soldier who survived a collapse in a bombed-out building recounted how he thought of his family at the moment of impact. That memory gave him the strength to remain conscious and crawl to a space where he could call for help. These personal testimonies make it clear that the will to live can push people to do what seems impossible.

Legacy of Hope

The miraculous survival stories of World War II remain a source of fascination. They show that while war is cruel and destructive, it also reveals the extraordinary resilience of the human spirit. People found ways to endure bombings, starvation, extreme weather, and injuries that should have been fatal. Families clung together in underground shelters, soldiers crawled through minefields, airmen drifted for weeks at sea, and children were pulled from crumbling buildings. Each story underscores a powerful truth: even when all seems lost, there can still be moments of unexpected salvation.

In many respects, these accounts also helped shape post-war societies. Survivors became symbols of hope, demonstrating that life could be rebuilt from the ashes. Governments sometimes used these stories in propaganda to boost morale during the fighting. Afterward, communities rebuilt around the memory of those who had beaten the odds. Monuments and plaques in European cities often mark spots where entire neighborhoods were wiped out except for one or two people who emerged alive. The war ended decades ago, yet these stories live on in family histories, memoirs, and archives. They remind us that, in the face of great adversity, the capacity for survival can be truly astonishing.

As we turn to the next chapter, which details peculiar prisoner escapes and tales from the camps, we will see a related aspect of survival under confinement. Just as these chapters share an overall sense of perseverance, the methods people used to break free from captivity also speak to the unbreakable determination that thrived in the darkest times of World War II.

CHAPTER 14

Peculiar Prisoner Escapes and Camp Tales

Prison camps during World War II became a second battlefield, hidden behind fences and barred gates. Soldiers, airmen, and even civilians caught in enemy territory faced confinement, often under strict rules and harsh conditions. Yet, even in these locked compounds, a spirit of defiance and ingenuity took root. Prisoners planned escapes with careful cunning, using homemade tools and forging documents that would fool the guards. In other cases, entire groups banded together to dig tunnels, create distractions, or stage elaborate deceptions to slip into the outside world. Some escapes became famous legends, while others remained quiet successes known only to those involved. This chapter explores these peculiar tales of captivity and the many escapes that happened despite security measures that were supposed to be unbreakable.

The Allure of Freedom

For many prisoners, the dream of freedom began the moment they were captured. Soldiers who prided themselves on fighting for their country felt a deep obligation to keep resisting, even from behind barbed wire. Airmen who had been shot down saw escape as a way to return to the skies and rejoin the war effort. Certain camps held men who had attempted escape multiple times, only to be transferred to higher-security facilities. This constant push-and-pull between captors and captives gave rise to a strange form of warfare behind prison walls, one that often relied on patience and stealth rather than guns or bombs.

Prisoners began to observe guard routines, studying patrols and shift changes. They learned the habits of the camp dogs, the layout of searchlights, and the times when the fences were watched more closely. Resourceful captives collected scraps of wood, bits of wire, and any fabric they could find. Old tin cans became ventilation parts for tunnels, while stolen electrical cords lit up secret passageways below the prison grounds. Forgery workshops sprang up in hidden corners, where men with artistic skills produced fake passes and documents complete with official stamps crafted from carved rubber or potato blocks. Others devoted themselves to sewing civilian-style clothes or even disguises that mimicked guard uniforms. Over time, these groups became highly organized, assigning tasks to each member based on individual talents.

The Great Escape

Perhaps the most famous operation was the one later nicknamed "The Great Escape," carried out by Allied airmen at Stalag Luft III in March 1944. Located in what is now Poland, the camp was specifically designed to be escape-resistant. The Germans believed they had taken every precaution, such as raising the huts off the ground so guards could check for tunnels. Yet the prisoners found ways around these measures. They dug three main tunnels, which they called Tom, Dick, and Harry, tunneling about thirty feet below the surface to avoid detection. They used bed slats to shore up the walls and built small rail systems to move dirt. They ingeniously disposed of the excavated soil by releasing it around the camp during daily walks, letting it spill from hidden pouches in their trousers.

On the night of the breakout, seventy-six men managed to escape through the most complete tunnel. The plan was to send as many as possible out of the camp, each with forged papers and disguised as foreign workers or civilians. Unfortunately, guards discovered the escape in progress, cutting it short. Most of the men who got out were recaptured over the following days. In a tragic turn, the Gestapo executed fifty of them, in violation of international law. Despite this heartbreaking outcome, the sheer scale and ambition of "The Great Escape" have made it a legendary event in escape history, demonstrating how far prisoners would go to regain their freedom.

Colditz: The Escape-Proof Castle

Another notorious site was Colditz Castle, an ancient fortress in Germany used to house high-risk escapees. Allied officers with a track record of breakouts were sent there, where thick walls, high cliffs, and a strong garrison seemed to make escape impossible. Yet the prisoners saw Colditz as a challenge. They tried nearly every trick imaginable: forging passes, hiding in laundry carts, and even constructing a secret glider in the attic. The glider project involved detailed planning, with men collecting wooden boards, fabric, and wiring from around the castle. The idea was to launch the aircraft from the roof, gliding over the river to safety. Although the war ended before the plan was put into action, it remains a testament to the creativity that flourished behind bars.

Some escapes from Colditz did succeed. One British officer managed to dress as a German guard and boldly march out with a group of actual guards. Others scaled the castle walls at night, risking fatal drops if their ropes made from bed sheets gave way. A few men disguised themselves as workers or maintenance staff, gaining access to areas beyond the normal confines of the castle. Even if they were caught, the repeated attempts forced the guards to keep tightening security. Prisoners sometimes joked that it was their duty to distract the enemy by making them devote resources to preventing escapes. It became a form of psychological warfare, with the Germans constantly worrying about the next cunning plan.

Harsh Realities in the East

On the Eastern Front, prisoner-of-war camps operated by both Nazi Germany and the Soviet Union were notorious for their brutality. Soviet prisoners in German camps faced starvation and disease on a massive scale, while German POWs captured by the Red Army also experienced terrible conditions. Despite this grim reality, escapes did happen. Some Soviet inmates dug tunnels through frozen ground or used brute force to break loose, though such attempts often ended in tragedy. The few who succeeded told stories of wandering across enemy-held territory, stealing or begging for food, and hiding in barns or forests. Winter weather could be a deadlier obstacle than any guard, and only the toughest or luckiest survived the journey.

In Soviet camps for German prisoners, vast distances and the harsh climate worked in favor of the captors. Attempts to flee sometimes meant traversing endless forests or snowy plains, with no clear route to friendly lines. Yet small groups did try, relying on stolen maps or compasses made from scraps. They carried meager rations, hoping to hunt or scavenge if needed. The entire war zone was chaotic, which gave them slim hopes of slipping through. Some had to turn back after realizing they could not survive the open countryside, but a handful claimed to have made it home by traveling mostly at night and avoiding main roads. Their accounts were often not widely publicized, but fellow inmates shared them in hushed admiration.

Civilian Internments and Resistance

Not all captives were military personnel. Civilian internment took place in Occupied Europe, in territories seized by Japan, and in other parts of the world. These camps held political dissidents, resistance members, or simply people deemed a threat by the occupying forces. The desire to escape was just as strong, if not stronger, for these civilians. Many lacked military training, yet they showed remarkable ingenuity. A French woman held in a makeshift prison in Paris once managed to smuggle out coded messages through a sympathetic guard, coordinating with outside resistance fighters. The result was a well-timed raid that freed several detainees, slipping them into the city's narrow streets. Similar breakouts happened in the Philippines, Burma, and elsewhere under Japanese rule. Resistance fighters would strike at night, cutting through fences and overrunning guard posts before disappearing into jungles with the liberated prisoners in tow.

In some cases, entire villages or communities rose up when they learned that neighbors had been taken to internment camps. They blocked roads, ambushed transport trucks, or sabotaged rail lines carrying prisoners. While not as detailed or large in scale as the major prison camp escapes, these local actions also played a role in rescuing people. Captors found it difficult to maintain total control when the local population worked together to subvert their authority. Even so, these rescues came with high risks. Failure could mean harsh reprisals against anyone suspected of helping the prisoners.

Trickery and Disguises

One of the most fascinating aspects of POW escapes was the use of disguises. Men with sewing skills turned blankets into coats or repurposed uniforms into civilian clothes. Some learned to speak enough German, Italian, or another language to pass quick questioning. A single accent slip, however, could undo the entire ruse. There were cases of Allied officers dressing as janitors or farm workers, carrying fake tools or pushing carts loaded with contraband. Others managed to produce official-looking papers, complete with stamps and signatures, all created in secret workshops. A typical day's walk outside the camp might lead to a quick inspection by a guard, so the forged documents had to match local regulations precisely.

There was also a psychological element in these ploys. Guards who believed they were dealing with civilians or fellow soldiers were less likely to ask too many questions if the impostor displayed confidence. This approach could fail if a more suspicious officer asked detailed questions about regiments or local addresses, but a surprising number of prisoners succeeded simply by appearing to belong. Some even rode trains filled with real enemy troops, quietly reading a newspaper or appearing tired from labor duty. Reaching a neutral border or a friendly zone then became the final major hurdle.

Tunnels, Raids, and Accidents

Though tunnels were the centerpiece of several major escapes, other methods involved direct assaults or simply taking advantage of external chaos. When Allied bombers targeted locations near prison camps, the confusion allowed some prisoners to cut through damaged fences. Air raid sirens and panicked guards sometimes opened a window of opportunity that would not have existed otherwise. This was dangerous, as bombs could also hit the camp itself. Nonetheless, men in these situations saw a small chance and chose to seize it.

Occasionally, local resistance groups arranged outside help. They might place a ladder against the outer wall at a certain time, or leave a vehicle parked nearby for a quick getaway. Some watchers on the guard towers were bribed to look the other way, though such deals were fraught with risk, as betrayal by the guard could lead to severe punishment. Even so, enough guards were disillusioned or desperate for money that prisoner escapes became possible through these clandestine arrangements. The captives who made it out with this kind of help usually disappeared into safe houses, changing clothes and forging new identities, then traveled by night to a friendlier area.

Unsung Heroes and Returnees

One unusual aspect of camp life was that not everyone left for good once they had a chance. A few men escaped successfully but returned with supplies or to help friends attempt a breakout. These stories sound unbelievable, but they highlight the intense loyalty that developed among prisoners. If someone had bonded closely with fellow inmates, they might not rest easy while those friends remained behind. Risking recapture by returning was a rare choice, yet it did happen. Sometimes they slipped in under the cover of darkness, delivering medicine or critical items that the camp lacked.

Other prisoners who made it out chose to rejoin the fight immediately. If they escaped in Europe and found resistance groups, they might stay to train partisans or gather intelligence instead of trying to go back home. This contributed to the war effort and boosted the morale of those still imprisoned, who heard rumors that their escaped comrades were fighting in the underground. On the other hand, some escapees were never heard from again, and it remained unclear whether they reached safety, were killed on the run, or died of exposure in a remote area. Camp inmates pieced together what information they could, sometimes passing along the story that so-and-so was last seen trying to cross a river at night.

Human Bonds in Captivity

Although escapes were a key focus for many, everyday life in the camps also involved forming close friendships and support networks. Men created small committees to plan escapes, divide rations, and organize distractions to keep the guards occupied. They might put on theatrical shows, celebrate birthdays with scraps of food arranged in creative ways, or hold secret religious services. Even the guards, at times, formed uneasy relationships with prisoners, especially if both sides had grown tired of the war. Some older guards turned a blind eye to certain activities, silently disapproving of the conflict and hoping for an end. Yet the core tension remained: the captives wanted to break free, and the guards were there to prevent that.

Legacy of Camp Tales

After the war, numerous books, documentaries, and films depicted prisoner-of-war escapes. These stories often struck a chord because they showed how the human desire for freedom could outwit even elaborate prison systems. Many of the real participants, however, had ambivalent feelings. Some were proud of their ingenuity but still haunted by memories of harsh reprisals or lost comrades. Families of those who died in escape attempts grieved the empty seat at the table, knowing their loved one died chasing the chance of liberty.

Governments studied these escapes to improve future security measures and also to learn how morale, leadership, and creativity could persist under oppression. The experiences of men at Stalag Luft III, Colditz, and other camps are still taught in some military academies as examples of psychological resilience. They show that even when a soldier is captured, the war does not necessarily end for him. The mind remains a powerful battleground, where hope and cunning can keep the fight alive.

Today, the remnants of tunnels, old forging tools, and small artifacts are preserved in museums or discovered by historians and enthusiasts. They stand as a testament to the extraordinary lengths that people went to escape captivity. Veterans who lived long enough to see these findings shared their recollections, pointing out where they once crawled underground or where they hid contraband in a false wall. For younger generations, these items and stories bring the war closer, illustrating that bravery does not always involve charging a battlefield; sometimes it means quietly working by lantern light to carve a path to freedom.

Prison camps remain a stark reminder that war imprisons not only the body but also the mind. Yet, in these peculiar tales of escapes and camp life, we see that the human spirit can resist captivity with a blend of humor, creativity, and determination. The next chapters will reveal even more facets of this vast conflict, continuing to highlight how personal stories could be as important as major battles in shaping the war's outcomes and its enduring lessons.

CHAPTER 15

The Home Front – Odd Happenings Away from Battle

When people think of World War II, they often imagine fierce combat on distant fields, massive naval battles, and dramatic aerial dogfights. Yet, much of the war's history took place far from the front lines. Across the globe, regular citizens lived under new rules and pressures that changed their daily routines in strange and unexpected ways. Rationing shaped meals, propaganda filled the airwaves, and entire industries shifted focus to produce weapons or supplies. Odd behaviors, secret rumors, and surprising social changes emerged in these home-front settings, where the war shaped everyday life just as surely as it did in the trenches or on warships. This chapter explores the peculiar side of life away from direct combat, revealing how the conflict influenced the simplest acts, from grocery shopping to neighborhood gatherings.

Rationing and Creative Cooking

One of the most striking effects on civilians in countries like Britain, Germany, and even the United States was the rationing of food, fuel, and other essentials. Governments introduced ration books and coupons, limiting how much of each item a person could buy. Suddenly, items that had once been readily available, such as butter, sugar, or meat, became scarce luxuries. Housewives, cooks, and even professional chefs scrambled to invent recipes that used substitutes. These dishes sometimes produced unexpected flavors and textures. In Britain, people used powdered eggs in baking, stretched small amounts of meat with vegetables and oats, or learned to enjoy carrots more than ever before. No one pretended these inventions tasted as good as the real thing, but they allowed families to stay fed under harsh conditions.

In Germany, rationing grew severe as the war dragged on, and the situation worsened when Allied bombings disrupted transportation lines. Families saved kitchen scraps, tried to make bread with unusual grains, and queued for hours to get the smallest portions of essentials. Rumors circulated about black-market deals, where those with connections could still get fresh fruit or meat, but at outrageous prices. Meanwhile, in the United States, rationing took the form of limiting gas, rubber, and certain foods, though America's vast resources meant civilians there never faced starvation. People still complied with "meatless Mondays" or "wheatless Wednesdays," seeing them as patriotic sacrifices that helped support soldiers overseas. Nonetheless, some Americans complained about the inconvenience and sought ways to cheat the system. Secret trade of ration stamps or hoarding became a small but noticeable issue, though the government tried to crack down on it.

Blackouts and Dark Streets

Air raids were a constant fear in many parts of Europe and Asia, leading to strict blackout regulations. In Britain, especially during the Blitz, authorities required that no light escape from homes or businesses at night. This meant covering windows with heavy curtains or paint, turning off streetlights, and ensuring that cars used dimmed headlights. Pedestrians stumbled along dark sidewalks, sometimes falling over curbs or bumping into lamp posts. There were stories of people painting their garden walls white or attaching strips of white cloth to their coats so they could see one another in the gloom. This darkness fostered a strange atmosphere, where neighbors could pass each other without recognizing who was walking by. It also led to unusual crimes, as thieves found it easier to slip around unseen. City dwellers adapted by carrying small flashlights with cowls that directed the beam downward, giving them just enough light to avoid obstacles.

In Germany, similar blackout rules existed, meant to reduce the effectiveness of Allied night bombers. Cities that had once been lively at night turned eerily still under the darkness. Some older residents recalled hearing only distant anti-aircraft guns or sirens piercing the quiet. Others took advantage of the dark to hold clandestine gatherings, especially if they disagreed with the regime. However, these were risky undertakings, since patrols roamed the streets and any light could draw unwanted attention. If a home showed even a crack of light from a window, neighbors might report it, fearing that the entire block would be targeted by enemy bombers.

Odd Jobs and Shifting Roles

Because so many men were drafted into military service, women took on roles that had traditionally been closed to them. Factories began hiring women to assemble aircraft, tanks, and munitions. Farmers relied on women to keep their fields producing food. In Britain, the Women's Land Army became a familiar sight, with young women in practical uniforms working farms and orchards. Rosy-cheeked from the outdoors, these new farmhands sometimes sang songs as they harvested or gathered hay, a stark contrast to pre-war norms. Even in countries like Germany, the need for labor meant women stepped into jobs once reserved for men. Some women later recalled these years with pride, saying they found a new sense of independence and skill.

In Japan, the situation was more complex. Traditional gender roles remained strong, but the prolonged conflict eventually forced changes. Young women helped produce fighter planes and ammunition in large factories, working long shifts. Students and older citizens were organized into volunteer groups to clear rubble after air raids or to help distribute supplies. Meanwhile, in the United States, the image of "Rosie the Riveter" became an icon representing women working in defense plants. Rosie's image, with a bandana on her head and her arm flexed in a show of strength, was part of a massive effort to recruit women to the war industries. Many responded, finding themselves operating heavy machinery, welding metal, or doing intricate assembly line tasks. Though some men resisted this shift, wartime necessity overshadowed older prejudices, at least temporarily.

Evacuations and Unlikely Friendships

In Britain and other countries under threat of invasion or bombing, many children were evacuated from cities to rural areas. Families in the countryside took in strangers' children, sometimes hosting them for months or years. This massive uprooting led to odd and sometimes touching pairings. A streetwise London kid might find himself living on a quiet farm, learning about milking cows or collecting eggs. Over time, children and their foster families formed deep bonds. Some evacuees cried from homesickness at first but grew to love the fresh air and open fields. Others never truly adjusted and ran away or stirred up conflicts. The government tried to keep track of everyone, but these large-scale relocations often fell into confusion, with children sent to places their parents had not expected. Many ended up writing letters home describing the odd animals and routines they encountered.

In Japan, as the war turned against the Empire, cities became targets for incendiary bombing raids. Families with means sometimes sent their children to the countryside to live with relatives or friends. Those who remained in the cities learned to take shelter in communal bomb shelters. Some of these structures were tunnels dug into hillsides. Others were simple concrete bunkers. Children forced to grow up in such an environment recalled nights of terror and days filled with chores to help the war effort. Despite the danger, small moments of friendship arose, such as neighbors sharing leftover food or teachers helping youngsters cope with stress. In these unusual circumstances, new bonds formed that might not have existed outside the pressures of war.

Rumors, Superstitions, and Wartime Oddities

War often sparks rumors and superstitions. Civilians found themselves believing strange tales or passing along gossip about secret weapons, hidden agents, or miraculous predictions. In some British towns, for instance, there were persistent rumors that the government had a stockpile of advanced bombs that would instantly end the war if only Churchill chose to deploy them. These stories had no basis in reality, but they provided comfort to people living under constant threat. Similarly, in Germany, rumor sometimes claimed that Hitler had supernatural advisors or was protected by mystical forces, explaining his earlier military successes. Though rational thinkers dismissed such talk, it circulated among the anxious population.

Certain behaviors also took on superstitious significance. Some families pinned sprigs of special herbs above their doors to ward off bombs, or they carried small charms they believed would protect them. Pilots had their own traditions, wearing lucky socks or refusing to eat certain foods before a mission. Sailors wrote the names of loved ones on the hulls of their ships. Even in neutral countries like Spain or Switzerland, citizens worried the war might spread, so they developed odd superstitions to feel safer. In these ways, people tried to regain control over terrifying events by clinging to rituals and stories that promised good fortune.

The Underground Economy and Bartering

Official rationing led to the rise of the black market, where goods were traded illegally at inflated prices. Some found ways to make a profit by buying up limited items and reselling them quietly to neighbors who had the money or influence to pay. In Britain, items like chocolate, stockings, or soap could become prized commodities. People sometimes exchanged personal belongings for a bit of real coffee or sugar. A woman might trade a spare coat in return for extra meat rations from a butcher who had access to local farms. Although governments cracked down on such deals, the black market thrived wherever the official supply system failed to meet daily needs.

In Occupied Europe, bartering became a way of life for many families. A farmer might secretly trade eggs and milk for a pair of boots made by a local cobbler, bypassing the ration stamps that no longer meant much. In the Soviet Union, entire markets sprang up in the shadow of official ones, where peasants sold produce directly or swapped goods with city dwellers. All sides recognized that survival often depended on bending the rules. Civilians in Germany found themselves quietly trading with foreign forced laborers or prisoners of war, risking punishment if caught. Yet desperation for food or clothes could drive people to take such chances. Newspapers sometimes printed warnings against participating in these illegal exchanges, while at the same time, the authorities struggled to keep track of every transaction.

Entertainment and Escapes from Reality

Despite the gloom, people on the home front looked for ways to distract themselves from constant stress. Movies, theater shows, and radio broadcasts became more important than ever. In Britain, citizens flocked to watch newsreels that showed Allied successes, cheering loudly when they saw victories on screen. In Germany, Goebbels's propaganda machine promoted films that glorified heroic soldiers or depicted cheerful families supporting the war effort. Even in the most bombed cities, cinemas tried to remain open. A simple comedy film or a piece of upbeat music could lift spirits for a short while, letting audiences forget the roar of planes overhead.

Radio played a huge role in shaping morale. Families gathered around their sets to hear speeches, announcements, and music programs. Comedy shows and radio dramas offered relief, although they were often sprinkled with propaganda messages. In Occupied countries, people risked severe penalties to listen to enemy broadcasts. Secretly tuning in to the BBC, for instance, could bring a sense of hope and a more realistic picture of the war's progress. Some families draped blankets over their radios at night to muffle the sound and kept the volume low so neighbors wouldn't overhear. In Japan, strict censorship meant that official radio stations rarely admitted setbacks, so citizens became adept at reading between the lines of broadcasts.

The Challenge of Housing and Displacement

Bombings and battles often destroyed entire neighborhoods, forcing people to relocate. Cities like Warsaw, London, Berlin, and Tokyo saw vast swaths of housing reduced to rubble. Families who lost their homes turned to relatives or emergency shelters. Schools, churches, or community centers served as temporary residences, crammed with cots and limited sanitation facilities. In some cases, the government arranged for evacuees to live in rural areas, as mentioned earlier. The constant movement of people led to overcrowding, the spread of illness, and frayed nerves. Disputes over living space surfaced frequently, with officials struggling to maintain order and fairness.

In Allied countries, the government sometimes commandeered grand houses or hotels to house displaced families or use as medical facilities. Owners might find themselves sharing their opulent living rooms with complete strangers. This mixing of social classes produced odd scenarios in which wealthy individuals had to adapt to a communal lifestyle. Conversely, poorer families sometimes experienced the relative comfort of staying in once-luxurious surroundings, though the experience was overshadowed by the tragedy of war. These temporary solutions seldom felt stable, and many families anxiously awaited the day they could return to their old addresses—if those buildings still stood at the war's end.

Civil Defense Volunteers and Local Heroes

Millions of ordinary people volunteered in civil defense roles, such as air raid wardens, firefighters, or first aid workers. These volunteers patrolled darkened streets during blackouts, enforced curfews, and rushed to sites hit by bombs. They were not professional soldiers, yet their tasks were dangerous. A single incendiary bomb could ignite an entire block, and it fell to volunteer fire crews to control the blaze. Some stories tell of brave wardens pulling people from burning rubble at the risk of their own lives. Others recall how neighbors formed improvised rescue squads, digging through collapsed buildings in search of survivors. Though not wearing military uniforms, these volunteers faced trauma and hazard nearly as great as any front-line soldier.

In places like the Soviet Union, local defense committees also handled distribution of rations, the guarding of supply depots, and the coordination of air raid drills. Elderly citizens and teenagers filled these roles because most able-bodied adults were at the front. They took pride in their small but vital contributions. A sense of community often arose in these groups, as they worked to protect one another. People who had once been strangers now cooperated daily in tasks like organizing communal gardens or setting up soup kitchens. This spirit, though born of necessity, forged bonds that endured even after the war ended.

Spies in the Streets

Cities not directly on the front lines also witnessed shadowy intelligence operations. Agents from both Allied and Axis powers tried to gather information about troop movements, factory output, or morale. Some spies posed as ordinary workers or refugees. A shopkeeper might notice a regular customer who seemed to pay unusual attention to railroad timetables. An office clerk might see someone copying certain documents under the guise of routine paperwork. Children, sometimes overlooked by adults, could be used to pass messages or observe suspicious activities. While much has been written about espionage in war zones, the home front also served as a battleground for secret operations.

Citizens learned to be cautious about sharing personal details or repeating rumors. Posters warned them that "Careless talk costs lives," encouraging them to keep quiet about troop movements, schedules, or personal stories that might reach an enemy spy. Some found the atmosphere of suspicion claustrophobic, especially when they realized that the quiet neighbor or the new coworker might be an informer. Yet the stakes were high enough that most accepted these restrictions. In Occupied countries, collaborating with the enemy could carry dire consequences. Even a whisper to the wrong person could result in arrests or worse. Meanwhile, genuine spies tried to blend in, forging relationships while carefully noting local gossip and official statements.

The Mood of Wartime Society

Throughout all these odd developments—rationing, evacuations, blackouts, and changing social roles—a sense of unity and endurance often emerged among citizens. Many believed that despite the sacrifices and inconveniences, their collective effort would lead to eventual victory or, at least, survival. Propaganda played a role in maintaining morale, but it was also everyday acts of kindness and shared struggle that kept people going. They joined queues without complaint, sewed patches onto worn clothes, and listened patiently to the radio for whatever news might offer a glimmer of hope.

Of course, not everyone accepted the hardships with a smile. Some engaged in petty crimes, profiteering, or black market deals. Others fell into despair, unable to cope with the strain. Yet the large-scale unity often seen on the home front became one of the surprising strengths of warring nations, showing that conflict was not solely about armies but about entire societies mobilizing behind a cause or at least struggling to keep daily life afloat.

In the end, the war's outcome was shaped not only by battles and technology but by how well each nation's civilian population held together under pressure. The strange events and stories from the home front stand as proof that large-scale conflict touches every corner of a country, altering the simplest habits in ways that can seem both remarkable and bizarre.

CHAPTER 16

The Power of Propaganda and Weird Influences

World War II was as much a battle of ideas as it was of bullets and bombs. Governments across the globe recognized that public opinion could drive armies and shape nations, so they poured immense effort into propaganda campaigns. Posters, radio broadcasts, movies, and even children's books carried messages urging people to fight, work, or sacrifice for their country's cause. In some cases, these messages seemed straightforward, such as calling for unity or denouncing the enemy as cruel. But other campaigns took strange or surprising turns, using odd themes, bizarre imagery, or manipulative strategies to influence minds. This chapter examines the ways propaganda shaped behavior and morale, as well as the strange twists and odd influences that sometimes emerged in wartime messaging.

Governments in Control of the Narrative

From the earliest days of the war, leaders understood the importance of controlling information. In Nazi Germany, Joseph Goebbels headed the Ministry of Public Enlightenment and Propaganda, carefully crafting messages that glorified Hitler's regime and demonized the nation's foes. Posters showed heroic German soldiers standing against weak or monstrous enemies. The government banned any artwork or news that did not align with Nazi ideology. Radios broadcast stirring speeches, while newspapers printed only officially approved content. Public rallies and ceremonies became grand spectacles, enforcing a sense of national pride. Over time, this constant stream of propaganda convinced many Germans that their war effort was just and necessary, although as the war turned against Germany, the gap between official claims and harsh reality grew increasingly stark.

In the Soviet Union, propaganda similarly glorified the Communist Party and Stalin's leadership. Newspapers and radio bulletins reported Soviet victories in glowing terms, downplaying defeats or blaming them on cowardice. Posters depicted brave Red Army soldiers fighting to protect the Motherland, often showing them side by side with workers and peasants. The concept of the "Great Patriotic War" emerged, rallying citizens to defend their homeland against the German invaders. Soviet propaganda also embraced themes of sacrifice and unity, portraying the war as a collective endeavor where every citizen had a role. Stalin's image appeared everywhere, building the idea that he personally guided the nation's defense.

In Britain and the United States, propaganda had a slightly different tone. Both nations emphasized democratic values and the need to defeat dictatorships. Cartoons and radio shows mocked Axis leaders, making them look foolish or evil. Recruiting posters, such as Britain's famous "Your Country Needs YOU" or America's "Uncle Sam Wants YOU," had already existed in World War I but returned with fresh energy. Governments urged citizens to buy war bonds, volunteer for civil defense, and accept rationing without complaint. While not as rigidly controlled as in totalitarian states, the Allies also managed the flow of war news, censoring reports that might harm morale or reveal military secrets. Political cartoons, songs, and patriotic films added to the sense that everyone was fighting for a noble cause.

The Strange Art of Posters and Cartoons

Posters became a primary weapon in the propaganda arsenal. Governments covered walls, fences, and public spaces with brightly colored images designed to catch people's eyes. Some appealed to national pride, showing flags or heroic soldiers. Others took a more bizarre approach, depicting caricatures of the enemy as rats or pests that needed to be exterminated. In Japan, for instance, posters sometimes showed Allied soldiers drawn with exaggerated, animal-like features, urging the public to see them as less than human. German posters often showed a giant swastika overshadowing a terrified Europe, implying Germany's power would bring order. Allied posters might show a cartoon Hitler being crushed under a rolling pin labeled "Victory," or a wide-eyed Japanese soldier being tossed into a garbage can.

Cartoons in newspapers and magazines offered another angle. They could be amusing, snarky, or downright vicious, all to reinforce a message. Some cartoonists gained fame or notoriety for their bold work. Readers found these sketches a quick, digestible way to absorb propaganda ideas. Children in particular were drawn to pictures, which meant many of these images were printed in coloring books or simpler forms, shaping young minds about who the "bad guys" were and why the war had to be won. Even subtle messages about saving scraps or donating metal found their way into cartoon form, with smiling characters reminding the public to do their part.

Radio's Grip on the Mind

Radio broadcasting was arguably the most direct way governments spoke to millions of homes. Speeches by leaders like Winston Churchill, Franklin D. Roosevelt, Adolf Hitler, or Benito Mussolini reached people sitting in living rooms or gathered in public halls. The power of these speeches lay in the emotional connection formed when a single voice addressed the entire nation. Churchill's call to "never surrender" or Roosevelt's "fireside chats" comforted and motivated citizens in dark times. In Germany, Hitler's addresses were carefully staged events, delivered at major rallies and broadcast nationwide, letting ordinary Germans feel they participated in a grand collective movement.

Yet radio also allowed for more subtle forms of influence. News bulletins, music programs, and dramatic readings mixed entertainment with propaganda messages. In the Soviet Union, radio plays glorified workers who doubled their quotas or soldiers who bravely fought in impossible odds. In the United States, popular shows took time to discuss war bonds, praising listeners who supported the troops financially. Even weather reports could be twisted, with forecasts omitting details that might help an enemy. Sometimes the simple act of hearing the national anthem at the start and end of broadcasts reminded people of their duty and unity.

Propaganda through radio also extended into enemy territory. Stations like the BBC broadcast news in multiple languages, hoping to reach Occupied Europe. Secret listeners, tuning in at risk, heard alternative accounts of the war. The Germans tried to jam these signals, but many people still found ways to listen. In return, Germany ran its own broadcasts aimed at Allied countries. Figures like "Lord Haw-Haw" (William Joyce) in Germany and "Tokyo Rose" in Japan became infamous for their English-language propaganda. Their programs mixed music and commentary, often trying to demoralize enemy troops by suggesting their cause was hopeless or that their loved ones were being deceived. While most soldiers dismissed these broadcasts as silly, some admitted they occasionally listened just for the music or out of curiosity.

Bizarre Claims and Magical Thinking

In times of great stress, people become more open to wild ideas. Governments sometimes encouraged or at least allowed bizarre claims to circulate if they served a purpose. In Nazi Germany, there was talk of "wonder weapons" that would soon appear to crush the Allies. Propaganda outlets hinted at secret research into super-tanks, death rays, or unstoppable rockets. Posters and articles suggested that even as bombs fell on German cities, a turning point was near. While some real projects like the V-1 and V-2 rockets did exist, many rumored devices were pure fantasy. Nonetheless, they gave hope to civilians facing dire shortages and constant bombing. By the time people realized these weapons would not materialize in large enough numbers, the war had already turned decisively against Germany.

The Soviets promoted heroic legends of partisans or soldiers performing miraculous deeds, sometimes hinting they were protected by an unbreakable spirit or special Soviet resilience. A single soldier might be credited with single-handedly stopping an entire German tank column. Though some stories had a grain of truth, they were often exaggerated or fabricated to show the Red Army's supposed invincibility. Similarly, Japan's propaganda stressed the idea that the Emperor's divine status would safeguard the nation, and that kamikaze attacks proved a spiritual might that Westerners could never understand. The Allies had their own tall tales, though generally more playful in tone, such as comedic depictions of incompetent Axis leaders or unstoppable Allied machines.

Hollywood and Film Propaganda

Movies were another potent vehicle for shaping opinions. Hollywood studios cooperated with the U.S. government to produce films boosting morale and demonizing the Axis. Actors and directors who had previously focused on light entertainment now created war dramas or documentaries. Stars like Clark Gable or James Stewart served in the military, and their status drew attention to recruitment drives. Cartoons by Walt Disney featured characters punching caricatures of Hitler or Mussolini, reinforcing a message that the Axis leaders were cowardly or foolish.

In Germany, the state-controlled film industry produced historical epics or musicals that subtly glorified Nazi ideals. Leni Riefenstahl's works, while made before the war, still influenced the cinematic style used during it. In the Soviet Union, directors portrayed peasants heroically resisting invaders. Japan also created wartime films that showed brave pilots or sailors triumphing over Western forces, though shortages of materials sometimes limited production quality. Audiences, hungry for distraction, often filled theaters. Whether consciously or not, they absorbed the messages embedded in these movies. Even newsreels shown before the main feature hammered home the official line on recent battles or political events. The dividing line between entertainment and propaganda grew blurry in many countries' cinemas.

Leaflets from the Sky

Both Axis and Allied planes dropped countless leaflets over enemy lines, hoping to sway soldiers or civilians. Some leaflets urged enemy troops to surrender by promising fair treatment if they laid down their arms. Others spread disinformation, exaggerating battlefield losses to undermine morale. Civilians in Occupied Europe sometimes found the leaflets scattered in fields or streets, reading them secretly. Occasionally, these papers carried coded instructions for resistance groups, mixed in with general propaganda. One of the most famous leaflet operations was the Soviet practice of dropping messages over German lines, inviting German soldiers to defect. In some cases, these leaflets had blank "safe conduct" passes that the enemy soldier could use to show Soviet forces they wished to surrender peacefully.

Leaflet campaigns often proved risky for the aircraft crews, as flying low and slow made them easy targets. Nonetheless, governments believed they could plant seeds of doubt in the minds of enemy forces or reassure conquered peoples that liberation was near. After major battles or bombings, leaflets might appear offering justification for the attack, claiming it was part of a bigger plan to hasten the end of the war. Civilians sometimes collected these strange documents as souvenirs, passing them around as curiosities or using them in household tasks when paper was scarce.

Cultural Influences and Subtle Shifts

Aside from direct propaganda, the war indirectly reshaped culture. Music, fashion, and language adopted wartime themes. In countries under rationing, clothing styles became simpler. Skirts grew shorter in some places because fabric was limited, though styles varied widely. The boisterous swing music of American bands influenced young people even in Europe, where listening to jazz was sometimes frowned upon by authorities. Secret "swing clubs" emerged in German cities, defying Nazi rules against "degenerate" music. In Britain, dances and tea parties took on a more somber feel, though many still tried to keep spirits high. Soldiers returning on leave brought stories, slang words, and gestures that filtered into everyday speech.

These cultural changes often came about in subtle ways, reflecting the tension between official propaganda and personal desire. A slogan on the radio might encourage everyone to remain vigilant, while the local dance hall tried to lighten the mood. People found themselves torn between fear of the unknown and the need to escape, even for an evening. The war's presence loomed in every conversation, shaping relationships and personal identities. Some youth embraced rebellious styles precisely because the government warned against them. Others became more conformist, trying to be model citizens in uncertain times.

Cracks in the Facade

Although propaganda was powerful, it had limits. By 1943 or 1944, many Germans saw that Goebbels's promises of final victory rang hollow. The sight of Allied bombers overhead or the knowledge that relatives were dying at the front clashed with official claims. In the Soviet Union, Stalin's regime continued to proclaim unstoppable advances, but peasants in devastated areas knew how much suffering still lay ahead. Even in the Allied nations, where optimism was generally higher, certain defeats could not be spun into success. Newspapers might downplay a military setback, but word of mouth often spread the truth among families who had lost someone in that operation.

Resentment grew when propaganda seemed too far removed from people's reality. Authorities found themselves fine-tuning messages, trying to keep morale from collapsing. In Occupied regions, the local population often saw through puppet governments' attempts to paint the Axis as benevolent. Underground newspapers and resistance radios gave alternative views. Secret jokes circulated about the absurdity of official claims. Yet fear of reprisals kept most people from outright defiance. Propaganda thus worked best when at least some portion of the public believed it contained an element of truth or a genuine promise of hope.

Post-War Revelations and Reflection

When the war ended, many were startled by how thoroughly they had been influenced. Soldiers returning home discovered that entire sections of their country's history had been manipulated or hidden. Civilians learned that official newsreels had often omitted key details about defeats. In Germany, the propaganda around the extermination of Jewish and other populations had concealed the true nature of concentration camps. Shock and disillusionment followed as the breadth of these horrors became known. Similarly, in Japan, people realized how severely the government had censored reports about Allied progress and the damage done to Japanese forces. In the Soviet Union, the state continued to control information even after victory, although some war stories eventually leaked out through veterans or foreign reports.

For some who had lived under totalitarian systems, the end of the war meant they could at last speak openly. They described how propaganda had shaped every aspect of their lives, from school lessons to street signs. Former youths recalled singing propaganda songs in class each morning, or memorizing slogans praising the leader. Allies also had to face criticisms that they had used manipulative techniques, though seldom to the same extent as dictatorships. Societies collectively questioned how such large-scale influence could happen. Many concluded that war naturally fuels propaganda, as leaders see controlling minds as crucial to victory.

Lessons in Persuasion

The propaganda experiences of World War II taught governments that words, images, and stories could be as powerful as tanks. The war cemented the role of mass media in shaping public opinion, a lesson that carried into future decades. Scholars studied the psychological techniques used, such as repetition, emotional appeal, and demonizing the enemy. Modern advertising, political campaigns, and social movements often trace some of their methods back to wartime propaganda discoveries. People also learned, on a personal level, that being too trusting of official sources could lead them to believe patently false narratives. Skepticism and the desire to seek multiple sources of information gradually became hallmarks of free societies.

Yet, even in the thick of war, individuals displayed pockets of resistance against propaganda. Some privately dismissed official broadcasts or found ways to tune into enemy stations, seeking a broader picture. Others drew subtle cartoons mocking their own leaders, risking punishment if caught. The interplay between powerful state messaging and personal experience was complex. Not everyone was easily fooled, but the constant barrage of persuasive techniques wore down many people's critical faculties, especially under extreme conditions. Observers looking back on World War II often marvel at how successful certain propaganda efforts were, while also noting the strength of those who refused to buy into government narratives.

Ongoing Influence

Decades after the war, historians continue to analyze posters, newsreels, and broadcasts from that era to understand how entire nations were mobilized or deceived. Artifacts like a tattered propaganda leaflet or a film reel showing a triumphant rally can still convey the mood of the time. Veterans remember how certain speeches inspired them to charge into battle, while civilians recall how they overcame fear by clinging to slogans that promised eventual victory. Although the literal fighting ended, these artifacts of propaganda remain a testament to the war's reach beyond physical combat.

As we move forward in our exploration of World War II, it is important to recognize that the war was not just a military event but also a grand theater of persuasion. People's hearts and minds were battlegrounds where governments, ideologies, and personal convictions collided. The "weird influences" of magical thinking, exaggerated claims, and highly emotional appeals were not sideshows; they were integral parts of a total war that demanded total support. Propaganda shaped morale, directed national policies, and even altered the cultural landscapes of the countries involved. In the chapters that follow, we will delve further into medical marvels, hidden treasures, and the final twists of the war, keeping in mind how these events were seen through the lens of carefully crafted messages.

CHAPTER 17

Medical Marvels and Curious Hospital Stories

World War II was not only about battles and strategic planning. It was also a time when medicine took huge strides forward. Doctors, nurses, and medics faced unprecedented numbers of injured soldiers and civilians. They treated wounds that ranged from ordinary cuts to serious burns from bombings, and they fought diseases that spread in crowded barracks or destroyed cities. Despite working under very difficult circumstances, these medical teams pushed the limits of existing techniques and invented new ways to save lives. This chapter explores some of the medical marvels and hospital stories that arose during the conflict—events that highlight both the challenges and the remarkable achievements of wartime medicine.

The Struggle on the Front Lines

Much of the essential medical work happened right near the battlefields. Field hospitals often consisted of large tents or hastily erected huts, placed as close as possible to the fighting so that wounded soldiers could receive immediate care. During the early days of the war, these facilities were sometimes overwhelmed, as armies had not fully prepared for the sheer scale of injuries. Doctors and nurses worked around the clock, short on supplies and facing a constant flow of wounded men. Blood loss was one of the biggest killers, so transfusions needed to happen quickly. At first, this required having donors nearby, but soon the method of collecting and storing blood in advance became more widespread. Donated blood was labeled and preserved in special containers, allowing medics to give transfusions at the front more easily.

Another major step forward involved the use of **sulfa drugs** (sulfonamides) and later **penicillin**. Sulfa drugs had been discovered before the war, but the conflict spurred their widespread use. They helped stop bacteria from spreading in wounds, drastically cutting infection rates. Penicillin, still in early development when the war began, proved even more powerful. By the later years of the war, factories in Britain and the United States were producing large quantities of penicillin, distributing it to armies worldwide. Suddenly, infections that would have been fatal in earlier conflicts were now treatable. Soldiers shot in the leg, for example, had a much better chance of survival because doctors could prevent or reduce gangrene and other complications.

Amputations remained common, especially for severe injuries caused by artillery shells or landmines. Even there, doctors tried advanced techniques, such as leaving the wound open temporarily to clean out infection before sealing it later. This approach, called "delayed primary closure," cut down on complications and sometimes saved limbs. The relentless pressure of war forced medical personnel to invent and refine these ideas on the spot. Despite the chaos, medical units managed to keep records of their successes and failures, passing on knowledge to others in the field.

Hospital Ships and Train Cars

Large navies often used hospital ships to carry injured sailors or marines back to safe ports. Painted white with large red crosses, these ships were supposed to be off-limits for enemy attacks, according to international rules. In reality, hospital ships sometimes faced danger. If an enemy suspected the vessel of secretly transporting troops or weapons, they might attack it anyway. Still, for the most part, these ships provided valuable care for wounded service members who needed longer-term treatment than could be offered by a temporary field hospital.

On land, hospital trains became a vital resource in Europe and parts of Asia. Fitted with bunk beds, medical supplies, and sometimes small operating theaters, these trains carried the injured away from front lines to better-equipped hospitals far behind. This was especially important in the Soviet Union, where distances were vast. A wounded soldier near Stalingrad might travel for days by train to reach a major city's hospital. In some cases, the tracks themselves were under threat from air raids or partisan actions, so these trains moved mainly at night or under heavy guard. Doctors and nurses onboard did their best to stabilize patients, handle emergencies, and keep detailed notes so that the next group of medical workers could continue treatment without confusion.

Strange Inventions and Surprising Tools

Desperate situations often call for creative solutions, and wartime medicine was no exception. Front-line medics sometimes improvised splints using rifle butts or pieces of wood from crates. They fashioned bandages from torn parachutes or clothing if official supplies ran out. In the Pacific, some American medics learned to use coconut water as a temporary substitute for IV fluids when nothing else was available. Although not perfect, it provided a solution in emergencies when no saline or blood plasma was on hand.

Engineers and doctors teamed up to design better surgical kits, portable X-ray machines, and even mini-laboratories that could be packed into trucks. This allowed doctors to diagnose infections or test blood types in the field instead of sending samples to distant facilities. The notion of "mobile medical units" became standard, with large armies assigning specific vehicles and staff to set up small hospitals anywhere they were needed. Many of these vehicles bore the red cross emblem, hoping to reduce the chance of being targeted by enemy fire, though in some intense battles that symbol did not always guarantee safety.

Civilians, Bomb Shelters, and Emergency Care

The Blitz in Britain, as well as bombing campaigns in Germany and elsewhere, placed huge strain on civilian hospitals. Air raids often hit residential areas, leaving hospitals overflowing with wounded citizens. Doctors and nurses relocated to bomb shelters or underground stations. They set up triage areas in subway tunnels or the basements of large buildings. Triage meant deciding who needed care first: those with the most life-threatening injuries, or those most likely to recover quickly if treated. It was a heartbreaking task, requiring medical teams to make split-second judgments about each patient's survival chances.

Civil defense volunteers, many of whom had little formal medical training, pitched in by dragging the wounded from rubble, bandaging cuts, and transporting people to whatever hospital still had space. Sometimes entire buildings were repurposed into makeshift medical centers. A school might be cleared of desks and filled with rows of beds. Some local doctors and nurses never left their posts, even if bombs were falling around them. Their bravery saved countless lives, although stress and exhaustion took their toll on these caregivers. Many wrote about sleepless nights and the emotional toll of hearing constant air raid sirens, never knowing if their hospital would be the next to fall.

Unusual Medical Cases and Heroic Outcomes

With so many people in conflict zones, doctors encountered medical situations that sounded almost impossible. Men survived gunshot wounds to the head if the bullet followed a lucky path. Pilots ejected from planes at high altitudes and were found with broken limbs but no major organ damage. Civilians buried in rubble for days were pulled out dehydrated but alive. The war forced doctors to expand their thinking about what was treatable or survivable. They devised new ways to handle extensive burns, using dressings soaked in special ointments, and they tested skin grafts to repair damaged tissue.

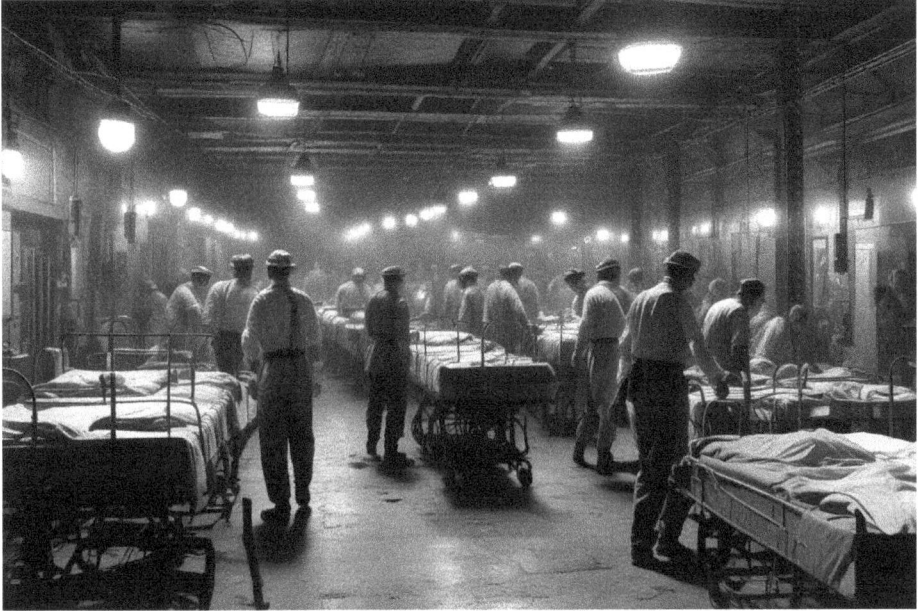

One remarkable story involved a soldier who was badly burned when his tank caught fire. He received an experimental skin graft procedure in which healthy skin from his thigh was used to replace the scorched areas on his arms. Though painful and slow, the procedure worked well enough for him to regain partial use of his hands. Another account described a child who had shrapnel lodged near the heart, requiring delicate surgery in a bomb-damaged hospital. The surgical team, lacking modern equipment, improvised with what they had, carefully removing the fragment and stitching the wound closed. The child not only survived but recovered fully, becoming a symbol of hope for the entire neighborhood.

Mental Health in Wartime

While physical injuries were visible, the emotional scars were sometimes overlooked. Soldiers returning from the front faced nightmares, flashbacks, and what was then called "battle fatigue" or "shell shock." Doctors recognized these symptoms more clearly than in World War I, but treatments remained limited. Some hospitals set aside wards for mental health, where soldiers could rest away from the terror of gunfire. Gradually, therapy sessions, rest cures, and some medications were introduced to help calm anxiety and sleeplessness. Yet, stigma around mental illness persisted, and many soldiers feared being seen as cowards if they admitted to mental strain.

Civilians also endured psychological stress. Constant bombings, loss of loved ones, and fear for the future led to widespread anxiety and depression. People coped by building community support or turning to faith, but professional help was not widely available. Some communities formed support groups, while local doctors tried their best to offer guidance. The war's disruption meant that mental health took second place to immediate physical needs. After the conflict ended, societies began to realize how deep the emotional wounds ran, prompting future research into post-traumatic stress and the need for better mental healthcare.

The Role of Nurses and Volunteer Aides

Nurses, often overlooked, were central figures in wartime medicine. Many were women who volunteered or were conscripted into nursing services. They worked endless shifts in hot tents or freezing barracks, tending to the wounded, assisting in surgeries, and offering comfort to those in pain. The war gave them new responsibilities and opportunities for leadership. Senior nurses managed large hospital units, trained newcomers, and organized complex supplies under the threat of air raids. In Soviet Russia, female nurses sometimes fought alongside infantry, dragging men from the battlefield under gunfire before giving first aid.

Civilians also volunteered in large numbers. In Britain, the **Women's Voluntary Service** aided bomb victims, while in the United States, the **American Red Cross** trained volunteers to staff hospitals and evacuation centers. Young men who were not drafted for other reasons sometimes served as orderlies, while older men or women too old for military service joined local hospital corps. This mass participation gave ordinary people a sense of purpose, and it meant that, despite the chaos, the wounded had a better chance of finding someone with basic medical knowledge.

Blood Banks and the Growth of Surgery

One of the biggest breakthroughs was the establishment of organized blood banks. Though the concept of blood transfusion was not new, it became a refined and systematic practice during the war. Donors from civilian populations lined up to give blood, proud to play a direct role in saving soldiers. Scientists discovered ways to extend the shelf life of stored blood by refrigerating it with an anticoagulant solution. Hospitals set up regional blood centers, shipping supplies quickly to areas that needed them. This improvement in transfusions led to lower death rates from hemorrhage, once a leading cause of battlefield fatalities.

Meanwhile, surgeons advanced their techniques at an astonishing pace. They pioneered methods for setting fractures with metal pins, operating on abdominal or thoracic wounds, and removing large foreign objects from the body. The stress of treating so many patients forced them to become more efficient. Some surgeons ended up specializing in certain procedures, developing expertise that saved lives daily. Their experiences became the foundation for modern trauma surgery. In places like North Africa, doctors battled not only war injuries but also tropical diseases like malaria, dysentery, and typhus. They recognized that controlling disease was as important as treating wounds. Vaccination campaigns and better hygiene reduced outbreaks that could cripple an army.

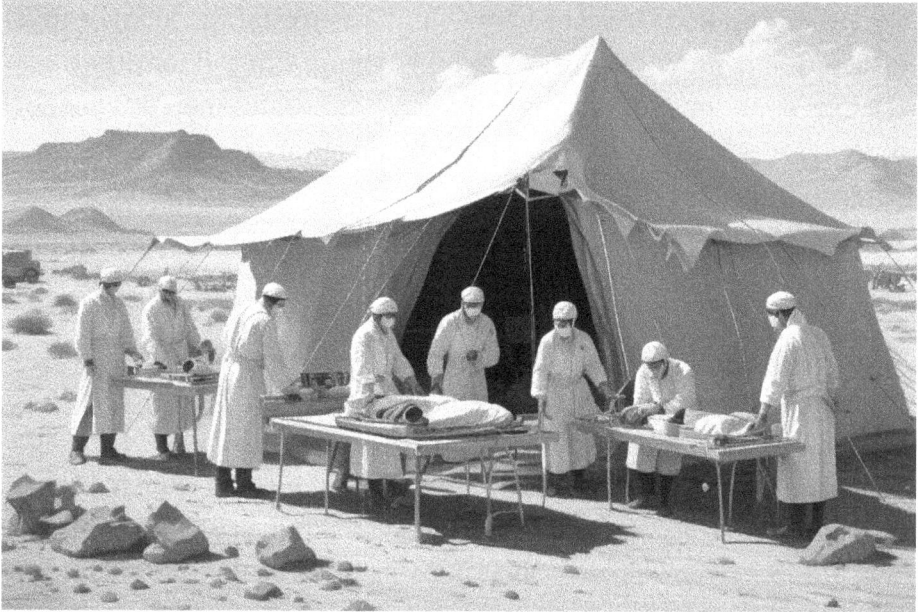

Stories of Hospital Rescues and Narrow Escapes

In the midst of chaos, some hospitals found themselves directly in harm's way. When the Germans advanced into the Soviet Union, entire medical units had to evacuate rapidly, taking their patients with them. Nurses and doctors loaded the wounded onto trucks or trains, sometimes leaving behind bulky equipment that slowed them down. They traveled day and night, trying to stay ahead of the front lines. Similar events occurred in Europe after D-Day, when Allied forces drove deeper into German-occupied territory. Field hospitals had to relocate to keep pace with the troops, ensuring the injured could be stabilized quickly.

One memorable episode involved a British hospital unit in Burma that was cut off by Japanese forces. Rather than abandon their patients, the medical staff organized a nighttime trek through the jungle, carrying men on stretchers for miles until they reached friendly lines. Local villagers helped guide them, offering food and shelter. Another account tells of a hospital ship narrowly escaping a submarine attack. Crew members quickly moved patients to safer compartments while the captain steered the vessel in evasive maneuvers. The torpedoes missed, and the ship made it back to port with all patients surviving. These tales highlight the courage of medical personnel who refused to leave their charges behind, no matter the dangers they faced.

Civilian Doctors and Secret Treatments

In Occupied Europe, some doctors risked their lives to hide or treat individuals targeted by the Nazi regime. Jews, resistance fighters, and escaped prisoners of war sometimes received medical care in secret basements or barns. Doctors and nurses had to keep these actions hidden from collaborators and local officials. If caught, they could be executed. Many used code names or false patient records to cover their tracks. Some bribed hospital administrators to allow certain individuals to stay under assumed identities. Although resources were minimal and the threat was immense, these covert operations saved hundreds, perhaps thousands, of lives.

In the ghettos of Eastern Europe, Jewish doctors worked under almost impossible conditions. Supplies were scarce, and the constant threat of deportation to concentration camps loomed. Yet they organized makeshift clinics, taught students in secret, and tried to contain outbreaks of typhus or other diseases. Their creativity in the face of misery is part of a larger story of resistance through medicine. Likewise, in parts of Asia under Japanese occupation, local physicians treated wounded civilians who had been caught in crossfire. They used traditional remedies combined with any modern drugs they could smuggle in. While official reports rarely mention these acts, personal diaries and testimonies reveal a hidden network of caregivers who took great risks for their patients.

Legacy of Wartime Medicine

By the end of World War II, medicine had moved forward in extraordinary ways. Techniques perfected under wartime pressure later became standard practice in civilian hospitals. Penicillin and other antibiotics found wide use, drastically lowering mortality from infections. Blood banks became routine, saving countless lives each year. Surgery for trauma victims was far more advanced, and the importance of hygiene and disease control in large populations was better understood. Nations also recognized the value of training more nurses and doctors, leading to expansions in medical education after the war.

Yet, the progress came at a terrible cost. Many physicians and nurses lost their lives in bombings, on front lines, or in concentration camps. Hospitals were destroyed, their staffs scattered. Civilians in Occupied regions endured horrifying conditions, and some medical experiments performed by certain Axis powers were inhuman. The war's end brought trials and condemnations for those who violated medical ethics. At the same time, doctors who had saved lives under incredible hardship were recognized as heroes. Their experiences served as case studies for post-war health reform. Documents like the Geneva Conventions were updated to better protect medical workers and facilities in future conflicts, at least in theory.

The stories left behind—of surgeons performing miracles with minimal tools, nurses standing firm during bomb raids, and entire hospital staff risking everything to save their patients—remain some of the most powerful and uplifting narratives of World War II. They prove that even in the darkest moments, humanity's capacity to heal and care for others can shine through. Medicine became a form of resistance to the destruction around it, a beacon of hope that lasted long after the guns fell silent.

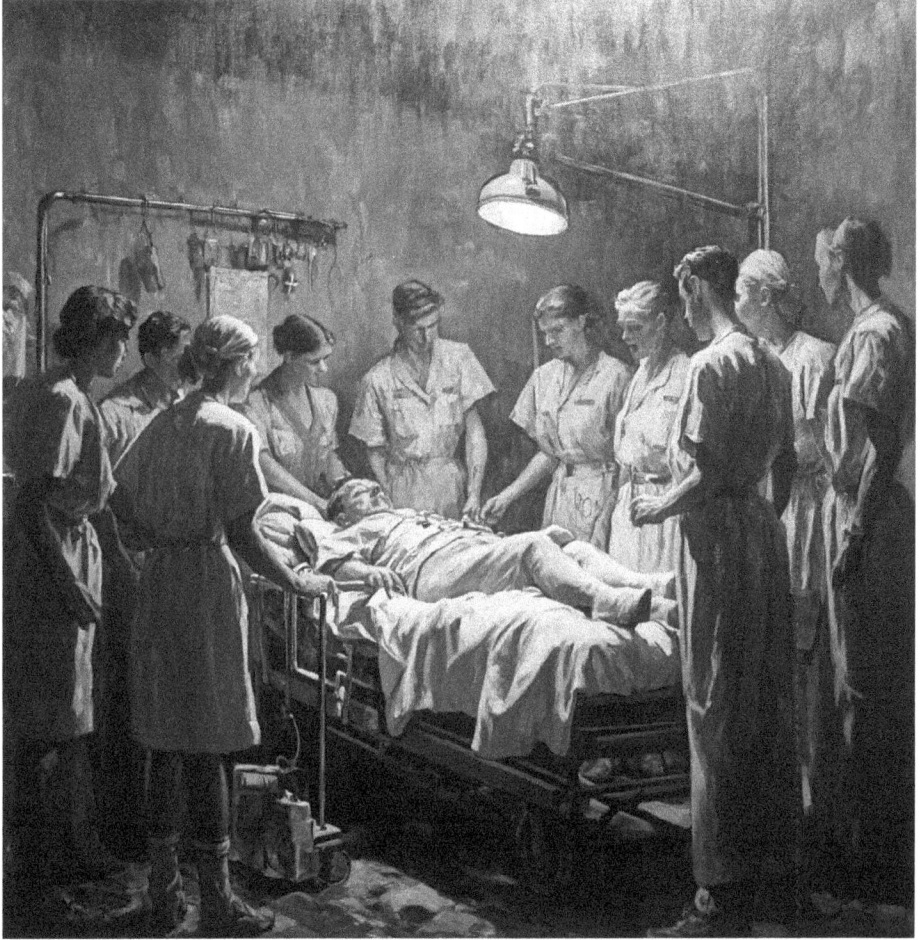

CHAPTER 18

Hidden Treasures and Strange Finds

World War II was not only a fight for territories and resources; it also led to the movement, theft, and hiding of countless valuable artifacts. Paintings, gold bars, rare manuscripts, and cultural treasures were shuttled around Europe and beyond, some vanishing into secret vaults or underground caves. Rumors spread of mysterious trains packed with loot, or submarines carrying precious cargo to distant shores. In some cases, these tales were exaggerated. In others, they proved very real, leading historians and treasure hunters on long quests after the war ended. This chapter dives into the strange world of hidden treasures during World War II, where art collections, royal jewels, and entire library archives sometimes went missing or were stashed away for safekeeping.

The Looting of Art and Culture

One of the most infamous aspects of the war was the systematic looting of art by Nazi Germany. Hitler and other top officials were deeply interested in amassing cultural treasures, both for personal collections and to establish grand museums that would showcase their idea of cultural supremacy. The **Einsatzstab Reichsleiter Rosenberg (ERR)** was an organization charged with seizing artworks from occupied countries, especially from Jewish families who were stripped of their possessions. Paintings by famous masters like Rembrandt, Vermeer, and da Vinci disappeared into the ERR's warehouses. Sculptures, tapestries, and rare books followed. In some regions, entire libraries were packed up and taken to Germany.

Countries like France, the Netherlands, Poland, and the Soviet Union suffered enormous cultural losses. Priceless pieces were taken from museums, private homes, and even churches. Some made their way into private homes of Nazi leaders, hidden away from public view. Others were stored in salt mines or underground bunkers to protect them from Allied bombings. In Austria's Altaussee salt mine, for instance, vast amounts of art were concealed, including works by Michelangelo and Jan van Eyck. Bombs were rigged in case the Nazis had to retreat, with plans to destroy the treasures rather than let them fall into Allied hands. Thankfully, local miners and some German officials prevented that final act of destruction.

The Allies' Hunt for Lost Art

Once the Allied forces understood the extent of Nazi looting, they formed special units to track and protect cultural property. Known as the "Monuments Men," these soldiers—often historians, architects, and museum experts in uniform—traveled with advancing armies, identifying stolen artworks and shielding important buildings from unnecessary damage. They followed leads from locals, interrogated captured Germans, and combed through hidden caches. In mines, castles, and abandoned train cars, they found paintings stacked like old furniture, sculptures wrapped in burlap, and crates labeled with faint hints of their valuable contents.

Recovering these items was only half the battle. Returning them to their rightful owners proved complicated. Some owners had been killed in the Holocaust, leaving no heirs. Others lived across oceans, meaning communication took time. In the chaos of post-war Europe, many pieces were misplaced again or stolen by opportunists. Over the decades, museums and private collectors have sometimes discovered that a painting in their collection was once looted. This has led to legal battles and efforts at restitution, with families trying to reclaim items lost during the war. The legacy of Nazi art theft remains an ongoing issue in the art world, reminding everyone how deeply conflict can reach into cultural heritage.

Gold Trains and Hidden Stashes

Stories circulated about trains loaded with gold bars, jewelry, and precious stones taken from banks or individuals. One famous rumor spoke of a "Nazi gold train" hidden in a secret tunnel in Poland. According to local legends, as the Red Army advanced in 1945, a train loaded with valuables disappeared near the city of Wałbrzych, never to be seen again. Treasure hunters and historians have searched for evidence of this train, using ground-penetrating radar and other tools. While occasional finds of tunnels or bunkers keep the legend alive, no confirmed discovery of a fully loaded "gold train" has emerged.

Other gold shipments were real enough. Germany seized gold reserves from occupied countries' central banks. In some cases, these gold bars were melted down, stamped with Nazi marks, and hidden in secret locations. Italy's gold also shifted hands when Mussolini's regime fell. The Allies, upon liberating territories, located caches of gold in caves or mines. A portion was recovered and returned to rightful owners, but the rest remains unaccounted for. Conspiracy theories abound: some claim that high-ranking officials used submarines to transport gold to South America, where it funded escape routes. Though some proof exists that Nazi officials fled with assets, the idea of massive shipments of gold crossing the Atlantic remains mostly speculation.

Yamashita's Gold and Pacific Mysteries

In Asia, Japan's wartime looting of treasures sparked its own legends. As Japanese forces advanced through Southeast Asia, they took gold, precious stones, and cultural artifacts from conquered regions. Rumor had it that this loot was collected under the command of General Tomoyuki Yamashita, stored in hidden tunnels or caves throughout the Philippines. The mythical "Yamashita's Gold" became a legend after the war, with numerous treasure hunters spending fortunes and sometimes lives searching for these hoards. Some claimed to have found partial stashes: gold bars or boxes of valuables. Yet nothing close to the vast fortune described in legends was ever confirmed.

Scholars debate whether large amounts of treasure truly remained hidden. Japan did ship enormous amounts of looted wealth back to its home islands, but U.S. naval victories made shipping more dangerous in the latter part of the war. Some believe the Japanese buried loot to avoid capture by Allied forces, possibly planning to retrieve it later. Others see the story of Yamashita's Gold as exaggerated or outright fabricated to attract adventurers. Still, the enduring rumors have drawn explorers to remote caves and mountains, hoping for a lucky strike. A handful of discovered caches suggest some truth behind the legends, though verifying the original source of each find can be difficult.

Priceless Manuscripts and Library Treasures

Beyond gold and paintings, many cultural institutions tried to safeguard manuscripts and rare books by hiding them from bombing or occupation. Libraries packed their most irreplaceable volumes into crates and sent them to rural monasteries or underground vaults. The British Library, for example, moved important items to secure locations away from London. The Hermitage in Leningrad stashed precious artworks and books deep in cellars to protect them from German shelling. In some cases, entire collections vanished into secret storerooms that only a few people knew existed. After the war, librarians and curators had to piece together where everything went.

Sadly, not all these treasures survived. Bombs sometimes destroyed buildings, losing centuries of knowledge in an instant. Fires ravaged libraries in Germany, Russia, and Japan, wiping out ancient scrolls and unique historical documents. In other instances, occupying armies burned books they deemed ideological threats. Still, some remarkable saves took place. When Allied troops entered Germany, they found hidden crates from universities across Europe. Careful documentation by local librarians allowed many volumes to be returned to their rightful owners. Over time, some libraries quietly discovered they possessed books stamped with foreign markings, indicating that these were spoils of war. Handling these items ethically and arranging their return or compensation continues to this day.

People's Personal Stashes

Wartime chaos led families to bury valuables in their gardens or hide them in attic walls. Some Jewish families in Occupied Europe, sensing danger, concealed jewelry or heirlooms in hopes of reclaiming them later. Refugees fleeing cities under attack sometimes sewed money or small treasures into their clothing.

There are stories of a grandmother's ring carefully hidden in the hem of a coat, only to be forgotten until years after the war. Although these personal stashes were smaller than the grand art hoards, they symbolized individual hopes for a future beyond the conflict.

In Eastern Europe, peasants sometimes discovered hidden belongings left behind by retreating armies or escaping families. A farmer might dig in his field and strike a metal box containing old coins or medals. Soldiers on the move often buried surplus ammunition or ration tins, though these were hardly treasures. Yet one might occasionally find a sealed container with valuables, stuffed away by a desperate owner. Attempts to track the original owners after the war were complicated if the rightful family had perished or moved abroad. Local legends sprang up around properties rumored to hold hidden gold, leading adventurous youths to crawl under floors or rummage through abandoned barns. While many were disappointed, a lucky few found something that served as a small window into the vanished world of the war era.

Undersea Mysteries and Shipwrecks

Not all hidden treasures lay beneath soil or in mine tunnels. The war put many ships at the bottom of the ocean, and some were rumored to carry riches. U-boats allegedly transported valuables from Europe to distant shores, though most documented U-boat missions involved military cargo, not gold or diamonds. Still, speculation persists about a few lost subs that might hold stolen art or Nazi gold. In the Pacific, Japanese vessels sank with looted goods aboard. Salvage operations decades later sometimes uncovered cargo holds filled with interesting relics, though precious metals were rare finds. The challenge of underwater exploration made it easy for rumors to persist.

Treasure hunters with specialized diving equipment took up the hunt, combing shipwrecks for anything of value. A handful of discovered items—like porcelain from sunken cargo or a chest of coins—fueled further stories. Yet the majority of these ventures recovered only rusted weapons, shells, or everyday supplies. The war's intensity meant that many ships went down quickly, and survivors rarely bothered with valuables amid the chaos. Nonetheless, salvage crews remain active in some parts of the world, hoping they might stumble upon a lost cargo of gold bars or a box of precious jade. Marine archaeologists, meanwhile, approach these wrecks as historical sites, more interested in documenting them than in seeking treasure.

Strange Post-War Claims and Hoaxes

The end of the war brought a flood of claims from individuals who said they knew the location of hidden bunkers or secret tunnels packed with Nazi loot. Some demanded money or equipment to reveal the spots. Governments in Poland, Czechoslovakia, and Austria often investigated these leads, spending resources to verify them. In many cases, the claims turned out to be hoaxes. People might have concocted stories based on local rumors or misunderstood references in old documents. Over time, officials grew skeptical of new leads, demanding concrete proof before launching costly searches.

A few actual discoveries kept hopes alive. In one instance, Allied troops found crates of gold dental fillings taken from concentration camp victims, stored in a remote Bavarian location. This discovery was grim proof of Nazi crimes rather than a romantic treasure hunt. Elsewhere, a stash of stolen silver candlesticks surfaced in an abandoned Nazi headquarters. Such finds demonstrated that, while rumors could be exaggerated, the practice of hoarding loot was real and widespread. Historians often worked with local authorities to piece together records, diaries, and eyewitness accounts to trace where these stolen goods traveled before disappearing. Decades later, families still occasionally uncover dusty chests in old houses, containing items looted long ago.

The Mystery of Missing Crown Jewels

Throughout history, crown jewels and royal treasures have fascinated the public. During World War II, certain countries feared an invasion would result in the theft of their regalia. The British royal family considered plans to move the Crown Jewels out of London if a German landing seemed imminent. In Romania, King Michael's government was rumored to have sent gold and jewels to a secret location, though the truth behind that story is muddled. The war's rapid shifts meant that governments sometimes rushed to protect their heritage. Belgium, for example, hurried its precious items out of the capital before the German advance in 1940, scattering them to safer spots.

Not all nations succeeded in hiding their treasures. Some smaller countries lost key regalia, never to be recovered. Stories of hidden royal jewels occasionally surface, with treasure hunters poring over old letters or diaries for clues. Most official records remain silent, either lost in the war or never kept in the first place. While modern technology—metal detectors, ground radar, forensic analysis—has improved the chances of finding hidden caches, success is still rare. The monarchy in a country that changed hands multiple times might no longer exist in the same form, leaving no official body to claim ownership if these jewels reappear.

Continued Searches and Modern Controversies

Even today, the hunt for World War II treasures continues. In some cases, it is driven by genuine historical interest, aiming to restore stolen art to families or museums. In others, it is fueled by dreams of untold wealth. Modern explorers sometimes clash with governments over excavation permits and ownership rights. Where items clearly belong to a museum or a known family, legal efforts may ensure restitution. But in many cases, the original owners died or have no direct heirs, creating complicated legal disputes. Some countries claim that any found treasure belongs to the state. Others allow finders to keep a portion. The moral and legal questions can be thorny, especially if the treasure's original acquisition involved war crimes.

Museums have also faced scrutiny about their collections, sometimes discovering that a painting or artifact was looted during the war. Efforts to research "provenance," or the chain of ownership, have grown. A painting might have official stamps on the back, or old receipts that hint at a shady transaction. Museums committed to ethical standards may voluntarily return such items or negotiate settlements with the families involved. Each case is unique, leading to a slow and sometimes messy process. Yet, these efforts underline how the war's shadow extends far beyond battlefields, affecting cultural heritage and the idea of rightful ownership decades after the conflict ended.

Reflections on a Hidden Legacy

The tales of hidden treasures during World War II offer glimpses into the desperation and greed that war can generate. Armies seized riches to fund their campaigns, governments hid national treasures to protect their identity, and ordinary people buried family heirlooms in a last-ditch hope of preserving what little they had. Some of these items were recovered, some remain lost, and others have turned up in unexpected places. Each discovery brings a mix of excitement, sorrow, and a sense of the past reaching into the present.

Behind every rumor of a gold train or a lost masterpiece lies a real story of lives disrupted by conflict. An artwork that once graced a living room might have been yanked away at gunpoint. A bar of gold could represent a country's entire economic security, stolen to finance an invasion. A battered suitcase filled with letters and trinkets might carry the memories of a family that never returned from the camps. In this sense, the search for hidden treasures is also a search for closure, a way to acknowledge both the cultural wealth that war displaces and the human stories entwined with it.

In the next chapters, we will turn our attention to the war's final phases—strange twists as the conflict neared its end and the lingering mysteries that were never fully solved. The hidden treasures we have examined are just one part of the puzzle, but they reveal how deeply war can penetrate into every corner of life, from the greatest museums to the smallest locked chests in an attic.

CHAPTER 19

Near the End – Strange Twists as the War Closed

World War II, which had started with swift invasions and bold strategies, dragged on far longer than many expected. By 1944 and early 1945, the Axis powers were being pushed back on multiple fronts. Germany faced the advancing Soviet armies from the east and the Western Allies—Britain, the United States, and others—from the west. In the Pacific, Japan's once-vast empire shrank under the constant pressure of American and Allied forces. Yet even in these closing stages, strange twists and unexpected events continued. Some of these moments came from desperation, others from sheer chance. This chapter examines the odd and surprising turns of the war's final months, when the Axis tried last-ditch measures and the Allies discovered that victory would come with hidden costs.

The Ardennes Counteroffensive

Perhaps the most shocking twist in the European Theater late in the war was Germany's Ardennes Counteroffensive, often called the Battle of the Bulge. By December 1944, Allied troops had pushed Germany out of France and were nearing the Rhine. Morale was high among Allied forces, and many expected the war to end soon. In a bold move, however, Adolf Hitler planned a large-scale surprise attack through the heavily forested Ardennes region, hoping to split the Allied armies and capture the vital port of Antwerp. German forces, including elite Panzer divisions, massed quietly. On December 16, they struck, catching many American units off guard in the dense winter landscape.

Heavy snow and fog aided the German advance, grounding much of the Allied air support. Confusion spread among American lines, as communications were disrupted and some front-line troops found themselves quickly overwhelmed. The sudden appearance of German soldiers speaking English and wearing American uniforms added to the chaos. These disguised enemy troops changed road signs, misdirected convoys, and sowed panic. Despite the German success in creating a "bulge" in the Allied front lines, a few determined Allied units, such as the U.S. 101st Airborne in Bastogne, held key crossroads. When the weather cleared, Allied planes attacked German tanks and supply routes. By January 1945, the German advance was halted, and the offensive collapsed due to fuel shortages and overwhelming Allied numbers. This final major German push, though ultimately a failure, was an unexpected turn that cost many lives and delayed the Allied march into Germany.

The Race for Berlin

As Allied forces closed in, a dramatic scramble began for control of Germany's capital, Berlin. The Soviet Union, having borne much of the war's brutality on the Eastern Front, was determined to seize Berlin before the Western Allies. Stalin wanted a political and symbolic victory, believing that capturing the city would give the Soviets a strong position in post-war negotiations. Meanwhile, Winston Churchill and Franklin D. Roosevelt were aware that whoever took Berlin would shape the immediate political order. However, Allied commanders decided the Soviet armies were better positioned to reach the city first, and the Western Allies turned to secure other strategic objectives.

Beginning in April 1945, Soviet troops encircled Berlin in a final, bloody battle. The city's defenders included not only the regular Wehrmacht but also young members of the Hitler Youth and older men of the Volkssturm (home guard). The fighting was fierce, with street-by-street and even building-by-building combat. Artillery and air raids pummeled Berlin's infrastructure. Some German units, lacking organization and supplies, fought on for the sake of protecting civilians or out of fear of Soviet vengeance. As the Soviets closed in, Adolf Hitler remained in his bunker beneath the Reich Chancellery, refusing calls to flee. He gave orders to non-existent armies and pinned his hopes on rumored miracle weapons. When it became clear that all was lost, Hitler took his own life on April 30, 1945. The German surrender in Berlin soon followed, though some pockets of resistance tried to fight on.

The fall of Berlin was far from a neat ending. Soviet forces discovered a city in ruins, with civilians hungry and terrified. Looting and acts of revenge occurred, though some Soviet officers tried to maintain discipline. The final surrender of German forces came on May 8, 1945 (May 9 in the Soviet Union), often referred to as Victory in Europe Day (V-E Day). But even as celebrations erupted in Allied nations, stories trickled out about the chaos in the defeated territories. There were also strange episodes of high-ranking Nazis attempting to flee or vanish, fueling rumors that some might have escaped justice.

Secret Negotiations and Rivalries

Behind the scenes, as the war drew to a close, secret negotiations took place among major powers. Although the Allies had agreed on a policy of "unconditional surrender," there were still discussions about possible deals with local German commanders who might surrender their regions without further bloodshed. In Italy, for example, German units signed an armistice with the Allies shortly before the official end date, speeding up the liberation of northern Italy. Meanwhile, in northern Germany, pockets of German forces surrendered to British or American troops rather than face the Soviets. Some German officials hoped these partial surrenders might lead to a split among the Allies, though their efforts ultimately failed.

Strange alliances or understandings also arose on the edges of the conflict. Partisan groups in Yugoslavia, Greece, and elsewhere had complicated relationships with the Allies, sometimes cooperating and sometimes pursuing their own political goals. The Soviets, British, and Americans all had different visions for post-war Europe, sparking rivalry and mistrust. Even as they cooperated to crush Nazi Germany, they were laying the groundwork for future tensions. Many local leaders realized that liberation from the Axis might be followed by the imposition of another form of control. In some areas, civil conflicts or proxy struggles began almost immediately, foreshadowing the shape of the post-war world.

Hitler's Alleged Survival and Other Conspiracy Tales

With Hitler's death announced shortly before Germany's surrender, rumors spread that he might have escaped. Witnesses claimed to have seen mysterious submarines leaving Europe, carrying Nazi leaders to South America. Documents describing sightings of "a man who looked like Hitler" emerged in later decades, fueling conspiracy theories. In reality, the Soviet authorities found partial remains in Berlin that they identified as Hitler's, though they kept details secret for years, contributing to speculation. Despite the official consensus that Hitler died in his bunker, fringe theories persisted, suggesting he fled to a hidden base in the Antarctic or lived under a false identity somewhere else.

Similar theories dogged other high-ranking Nazis. Martin Bormann, one of Hitler's closest aides, vanished in the chaos of Berlin's last days, leading to endless gossip about his whereabouts. Decades later, remains discovered near the site of heavy fighting in Berlin were identified as Bormann's, ending most speculation. But for a long time, these mysteries gave rise to rumors of "Nazi enclaves" far from Europe. Although historians largely dismiss the idea of entire secret Nazi colonies, a few war criminals did manage to slip away to places like Argentina and were only found many years after the war, proving that truth can sometimes align with the strangest rumors.

Japan's Final Stand

While Nazi Germany collapsed in May 1945, Japan fought on, even though its strategic position was dire. Allied forces had retaken much of the Pacific and were closing in on the Japanese home islands. Yet surrender seemed unthinkable to many in the Japanese leadership, who believed in the code of bushido and pledged to defend the Emperor to the last. The Allies launched devastating firebombing raids on Japanese cities, including Tokyo. These bombings caused massive civilian casualties and destroyed entire urban centers. Still, the Japanese government hesitated, hoping for a negotiated peace or some miraculous turn.

In July 1945, the Allies issued the Potsdam Declaration, demanding Japan's unconditional surrender. The Japanese government's official response was ambiguous, partly because of internal divisions. The war's strangest and most horrifying twist came in August 1945, when the United States dropped atomic bombs on Hiroshima (August 6) and Nagasaki (August 9). The sheer destructive power of these new weapons shocked the world. Japan's leaders confronted the reality that further resistance would lead to the annihilation of their nation. On August 15, 1945, Emperor Hirohito announced Japan's surrender, though a few military officers tried briefly to stage a coup to prevent it. Ultimately, Japan formally surrendered on September 2, 1945, ending World War II in the Pacific. The use of atomic bombs remains one of the war's most debated choices, raising moral questions about civilian casualties and the dawn of the nuclear age.

Mysteries in the Pacific

Just as in Europe, the final days of the Pacific war had their share of odd occurrences. Some Japanese soldiers, stationed on remote islands, continued to fight long after their homeland's surrender. Cut off from communications, they refused to believe the war was over. Stories emerged years or even decades later of Japanese holdouts. One soldier in particular, Hiroo Onoda, held out in the Philippines until 1974, insisting he needed official orders before laying down his arms. These tales highlight how the end of the war was not as clean and sudden as official surrender documents suggest. In many places, local conditions, personal convictions, and the lack of reliable information led to isolated pockets of continued hostility.

Additionally, the final weeks saw desperate Japanese strategies, including a wave of **kamikaze** attacks on Allied ships. Pilots volunteered or were ordered to fly their planes directly into enemy vessels, believing their sacrifice might slow the Allied advance. Although these attacks inflicted serious damage, they could not change Japan's overall situation. Some kamikaze missions were carried out by small or improvised aircraft, even piloted rockets. Despite their terrifying nature, these final attempts revealed how far Japan's leadership would go to avoid surrender. In the end, massive destruction and the threat of further atomic bombings forced Japan to accept the inevitable.

Collaboration and Betrayal

As the Axis powers crumbled, collaborators in occupied countries faced reckonings. People who had cooperated with Nazi or Japanese authorities sometimes fled, fearing vengeance from their fellow citizens. In France, the Netherlands, and elsewhere, mobs attacked suspected collaborators, often shaving their heads or parading them through the streets. In Eastern Europe, shifting lines of control meant that those who had welcomed the Germans when they arrived might now be persecuted by returning Soviet forces. Some communities found themselves bitterly divided over who had resisted and who had cooperated. Trials were held to punish high-profile collaborators, but many lesser figures blended back into society. This aftermath caused new social rifts, overshadowing the official joy of liberation.

Certain parts of Eastern Europe saw fluid alliances. Groups that had fought the Nazis might be declared enemies by the new Soviet-backed governments. For example, the Polish Home Army had resisted Germany, yet after the war, many of its leaders were arrested by the communist regime. Similar dynamics occurred in the Baltic states, where anti-Soviet partisans went on fighting in the forests, hoping the Western Allies might come to their aid. This complicated picture meant that the final stage of the war was not simply about defeating the Axis but also about shaping the political future of entire regions, sometimes in ways that felt like new oppression rather than liberation.

Unexpected Refugees and Displaced Persons

The end of the war unleashed an enormous wave of displaced persons—POWs, forced laborers, concentration camp survivors, and civilians fleeing battle zones. Many had nowhere to return, as their homes were destroyed or in enemy-held territory. The Allies set up displaced-person camps across Europe, where people of various nationalities mingled in temporary facilities, awaiting help. Families were separated by front lines or deportations, and parents searched desperately for missing children. Some Germans also fled westward to escape Soviet occupation, creating a massive refugee crisis. In Asia, displaced Chinese, Koreans, and Southeast Asians tried to rebuild their lives after Japanese rule ended, though resources were scarce and entire cities lay in ruins.

The chaos of these movements led to some bizarre situations. Former soldiers of different armies found themselves in the same camp, forced to coexist under Allied supervision. Concentration camp survivors, weakened and traumatized, struggled to trust any system that assigned them to yet another fenced-in facility, even if it was meant for their protection. Meanwhile, Allied authorities lacked the manpower and clear policies to handle millions of uprooted people. Some individuals used forged documents to claim different nationalities, hoping for a better chance at resettlement. Others ended up in the wrong country altogether, stuck in bureaucratic limbo. This post-war displacement was one of the largest migrations in history, spanning from 1945 well into the late 1940s.

Sudden Surrenders and Pockets of Resistance

Even after Germany's official surrender, scattered German units held out in places like Norway's northern reaches or the Channel Islands. Communications were patchy, and some commanders refused to believe the leadership's orders. In the Pacific, Japanese garrisons on isolated islands might not learn of the surrender for weeks, living off dwindling supplies. Allied ships and planes occasionally encountered these outposts, leading to brief skirmishes before the defenders realized the war had ended. Meanwhile, in China, the surrender of Japanese forces in various provinces created a complex situation, as rival Chinese factions rushed to claim territories. In some cases, Japanese troops actually kept local order until Chinese forces arrived, a surreal arrangement that blended the lines between enemy and caretaker.

This patchwork of local surrenders showed how complicated and uneven the final phase of the war was. The official ceremonies, such as the signing aboard the USS Missouri in Tokyo Bay, did not instantly switch off the fighting in every corner. Some Allied soldiers and civilians died in scattered incidents that took place after the main surrender dates. For them, the war's final chapter came too late. Over time, these stories of isolated battles became part of local lore, emphasizing how large-scale wars can continue in small pockets even when leaders have declared them finished.

Scientific and Technological Surprises

As the conflict wound down, Allied forces discovered secret Axis research facilities. Germany's rocket program at Peenemünde, which had produced the V-1 and V-2 missiles, came under Allied control. Scientists like Wernher von Braun and his team surrendered to the Americans, leading to the eventual transfer of rocket technology to the United States. Similar efforts occurred with jet airplanes, advanced submarines, and chemical weapons. The Soviets also captured German scientists, attempting to harness their expertise for Soviet projects. This fierce competition for Axis technology laid the groundwork for the post-war scientific race, although that is a topic belonging to later times.

Japan, too, had pursued unusual weapons, including balloon bombs that rode high-altitude winds toward North America. With the war's end, Allied intelligence teams uncovered partial plans for other advanced projects, some of them borderline fantasies. These findings showed that in their desperation, the Axis had been willing to invest in radical ideas. Many of these projects never saw the battlefield, but they became curiosities that historians studied afterward. The final months of the war, therefore, revealed not only the human toll of destruction but also the surprising leaps in military research that had occurred behind closed doors.

The War's Unpredictable Endgame

No matter how thoroughly the Allies planned, the war's ending was marked by confusion, last-minute deals, and emotional outbursts. Soldiers who had fought for years discovered that victory felt more like exhaustion than celebration. Civilians emerging from ruins struggled to rebuild. The revelations of concentration camps, mass graves, and the use of atomic bombs brought a profound sense of shock. Diplomatic friction among the Allies made the shape of the post-war world look uncertain and sometimes threatening. While the formal surrenders in Europe and Asia ended the active fighting, they also set up a new era of tensions that would define the decades to come.

Yet, the strangest part of these final twists might be how quickly everyday people tried to move on. In liberated capitals, parades broke out, couples danced in the streets, and children waved flags. At the same time, hidden under that celebration were all the scars of war—missing family members, bombed houses, rationing continuing for years, and an undercurrent of fear about the future. Many soldiers who came home found their neighborhoods changed, and some could not readjust. The illusions of the 1930s had vanished, replaced by a new awareness of how fragile peace could be. The war's last months showed that even as it drew to a close, conflict could still offer unexpected turns, each with a human cost that would ripple into the next generation.

CHAPTER 20

Aftermath and Unresolved Mysteries

When the final weapons fell silent in 1945, the largest and most destructive war in history had officially ended. Yet for millions around the world, the consequences of World War II lived on. Nations emerged as victors or the defeated, but individuals carried scars—physical, emotional, and spiritual. Families discovered that a return to normal life was far from immediate. Cities lay in ruins, economies were shattered, and political tensions simmered just below the surface. In this final chapter, we examine the aftermath of World War II and the unresolved mysteries that continued to haunt governments, historians, and ordinary people. These lingering questions reminded everyone that war's impact can stretch far beyond official surrender ceremonies.

Rebuilding Amid the Ruins

One of the greatest tasks after the war was the rebuilding of devastated cities. Berlin, Warsaw, Stalingrad (Volgograd), Tokyo, and many other urban centers had been almost completely destroyed by bombing or ground battles. Families returned to find only rubble where their homes once stood. Governments across Europe and Asia launched ambitious reconstruction programs. The Marshall Plan, introduced by the United States in 1947, offered financial aid to war-torn European countries, helping them rebuild infrastructure and revitalize industry. In the Soviet-occupied zones, reconstruction took place under a communist system that prioritized heavy industry, often at the expense of consumer goods.

Citizens volunteered in large numbers to clear debris, sometimes using simple tools or even bare hands. Women and older men played a key role, as many young men had been killed or were still in military service. Over time, major cities rose from the rubble, but the scars remained visible for decades. Some areas chose to preserve certain ruins as memorials, while others aimed to erase all traces of war damage. In Japan, the post-war American occupation led to massive political and social changes, rewriting the constitution and demilitarizing the nation. Yet for every shining new building, there were countless personal stories of loss, displacement, and painful memories that no amount of construction could fully replace.

War Crimes Trials and Justice

One of the most public aftermath events was the series of war crimes trials, meant to hold high-ranking Axis leaders accountable. The Nuremberg Trials in Germany, starting in late 1945, judged prominent Nazis for crimes against peace, war crimes, and crimes against humanity—terms that gained legal weight during these proceedings. Figures like Hermann Göring, Rudolf Hess, and Joachim von Ribbentrop faced international judges. The Soviets, Americans, British, and French provided prosecutors and legal teams. Evidence of genocide and mass murder shocked the public, as details of the Holocaust were laid out in official proceedings. Some defendants showed remorse, others denied responsibility, and a few insisted they were only following orders. In the end, several received death sentences, while others got lengthy prison terms or were acquitted due to insufficient proof of individual guilt.

Similar trials took place in Japan, where the International Military Tribunal for the Far East dealt with Japanese leaders accused of waging aggressive war and allowing atrocities. Emperor Hirohito, though deeply involved in wartime decisions, was not tried, partly due to Allied strategies for Japan's post-war stability. This decision was controversial, leaving questions about responsibility for the war's many horrors. Lower-level trials occurred across Asia, judging Japanese officers and soldiers for brutal treatment of POWs and civilians. Many were executed or imprisoned, though again some managed to avoid capture or punishment. Even in Allied countries, a few officials faced scrutiny for their own conduct, though most Allied leaders escaped serious legal challenges. The war crimes trials aimed to bring closure, but they also sparked debates about "victor's justice," as some believed the trials ignored wrongdoing by Allied forces or other complexities of the conflict.

The Fate of POWs and Missing Persons

Millions of prisoners of war had been held by all sides, and their post-war fates varied widely. Soviet POWs freed from German camps sometimes returned to suspicion in the Soviet Union, treated as traitors for having been captured. Many ended up in Soviet labor camps under accusations of collaborating with the enemy. German POWs in Soviet hands faced years of hard labor rebuilding cities. Some were not repatriated until the early 1950s. Meanwhile, Allied POWs returned home to heroes' welcomes, though they often struggled with trauma and poor health.

Beyond POWs, countless families searched for missing relatives. In the chaos of the war's final months, many soldiers and civilians disappeared without a trace. The Red Cross and other agencies tried to match up names with camp registers, hospital records, or prisoner lists. Some individuals had lost contact with loved ones years before and learned only gradually of their death or survival. Children orphaned by the war ended up in large adoption programs or lived in crowded orphanages. Countries like Poland saw entire new population shifts, as borders moved westward and families were displaced. These demographic changes meant that looking for a missing person could mean searching across what now belonged to a different nation. Though official "missing" lists shrank over time, many families never discovered the fate of their relatives, leaving them in a permanent state of uncertainty.

Cold War Shadows and Divided Lands

The alliance that had defeated Nazi Germany soon cracked under political differences, leading to the start of the Cold War. The Soviet Union tightened its grip on Eastern Europe, setting up communist governments in Poland, Hungary, Romania, and other states. The Western Allies oversaw the establishment of democratic regimes in West Germany, Italy, and parts of Austria. The old unity that had held against Hitler dissolved, replaced by suspicion and ideological conflict. Germany itself was split into occupation zones, which evolved into the separate states of West Germany and East Germany. Berlin became a focal point of this divide, physically divided years later by the Berlin Wall.

In Asia, the war's end saw the Chinese Civil War resume, leading to the communist victory under Mao Zedong in 1949. Korea, once ruled by Japan, was divided into Soviet and American zones, setting the stage for the Korean War in the early 1950s. Japan's transformation, guided by the American occupation, turned it into a pacifist nation with a new constitution, yet many in neighboring countries were uneasy about whether the root causes of militarism had been fully addressed. The swirl of shifting alliances, newly drawn borders, and the rapid onset of the nuclear arms race all had roots in the post-World War II settlements. Thus, while the war had officially ended, it triggered a fresh set of global tensions.

The Holocaust's Lingering Questions

Perhaps the greatest unresolved mystery and sorrow lay in the wake of the Holocaust. The scale of genocide against Jews, as well as the persecution of Roma, Poles, disabled individuals, homosexuals, and political dissidents, raised profound questions about humanity's capacity for evil. Even after the revelations of the concentration and extermination camps, many found it hard to grasp how such atrocities had been planned and carried out. Survivors struggled with guilt, grief, and the challenge of rebuilding lives with no surviving family. Some tried to emigrate to places like Palestine (later Israel) or the United States, seeking a new beginning. Others remained in Europe, forging communities with fellow survivors.

A key mystery was the fate of stolen belongings and stolen identities. Nazi officials had confiscated everything from personal photo albums to wedding rings. While some items were recovered, others vanished into black markets or hidden caches. Even decades later, families that survived discovered old records or documents hinting at lost property. Legal battles over these claims sometimes lasted generations. Meanwhile, historians pieced together diaries, letters, and testimonies, wrestling with the horror of how ordinary people had participated in genocide. The search for any surviving clues about missing individuals continued, with many families never learning the details of their loved ones' final hours.

War's Shadow on Technology and Science

Although World War II ended, its technological legacy persisted. Military research had produced innovations in rocketry, jet propulsion, radar, and computing. Scientists who once worked for the Axis found themselves courted by Allied powers. Operation Paperclip, conducted by the United States, secretly transported German scientists—including rocket experts—to America. The Soviet Union ran similar programs, hoping to harness these brains to bolster its own scientific projects. This rush led to questions about moral compromise. Some of these scientists had links to Nazi ideology or experiments in forced labor camps, raising the issue of whether using their expertise effectively rewarded criminal behavior.

The dawn of the atomic age presented another profound dilemma. The bombs dropped on Hiroshima and Nagasaki demonstrated nuclear power's destructive capability. Governments worldwide realized that future wars could be even more catastrophic if nuclear weapons were used. Yet, the Cold War rivalry spurred an arms race, with both the United States and the Soviet Union determined to build more powerful arsenals. Scientists who had helped create the bomb wrestled with guilt and warnings about potential annihilation. Thus, while the war's official battles had ceased, its technological momentum led humanity into a new era of threats, overshadowing any sense of relief that peace might otherwise have brought.

Investigations of High-Level Secrets

Even as the war ended, many top-secret projects and intelligence operations remained undisclosed. Governments sorted through captured documents, trying to understand the full extent of Axis espionage and sabotage. Documents revealed that German and Japanese codebreakers had worked aggressively but with mixed success. Some records described planned operations that never occurred, such as a proposed Japanese strike on the Panama Canal or a German scheme to bomb New York using long-range missiles. Not all these ideas were feasible, but their existence highlighted how wide the war's scope might have become.

In some cases, Allied officials withheld certain details to keep strategic advantages or to avoid embarrassing revelations about their own methods. The Ultra secret—that the Allies had broken German Enigma codes—was kept tight for decades, with only select insiders aware of how vital codebreaking had been. Meanwhile, the Soviets refused to release certain records that might clarify events like the Katyn Massacre, fueling speculation and anger in Poland and the West. These hidden chapters of the war ensured that historians would spend years piecing together the truth, sometimes challenging official narratives.

Veterans and their Return

Millions of servicemen and women demobilized, returning to civilian life with uncertain prospects. Some found jobs quickly in factories or businesses that were shifting from war production to peacetime goods. Others struggled with injuries, both physical and mental, and discovered that the governments they had served were slow to provide adequate support. In the United States, the G.I. Bill offered education benefits and housing loans, easing the transition for many veterans. In contrast, Soviet soldiers returned to a land ravaged by war, with entire towns and villages erased from the map.

In Britain, the economy remained weak, and rationing continued well into the late 1940s. The sense of relief at surviving the Blitz and winning the war mixed with frustration about ongoing shortages. In Germany, returning soldiers often found themselves scorned or pitied, as the new Allied-occupied government tried to distance itself from Nazi policies. Japanese veterans faced a society in which the Emperor's divinity was questioned, and the entire structure of national pride had been shaken. Across all nations, families had to rebuild relationships. Children barely recognized fathers who had been gone for years, and couples discovered that wartime experiences had changed them, sometimes leading to tensions or divorce. Though victory parades happened, they did not erase the complexity of returning home.

The Long Road of Memorials and Remembrance

As the dust settled, communities began to create memorials to the dead. Monuments, plaques, and war cemeteries appeared in every country involved in the conflict. Some families erected private tombstones without an actual body to bury, using symbolic graves for those declared missing in action. Others contributed funds to build community halls or libraries dedicated to fallen soldiers' names. Military cemeteries in places like Normandy or Arlington became sites of annual remembrance ceremonies. Pilgrimages to former battlefields grew in popularity, with veterans returning to pay respects or find closure.

This process of remembrance sparked debates. Some groups insisted on acknowledging all victims, including civilians and persecuted minorities. Others wanted to highlight only patriotic sacrifices. In newly formed communist states, the war's memory was harnessed for propaganda, glorifying the Red Army's role above all else. In Western countries, the Holocaust gradually became central to the war's narrative, leading to Holocaust education programs and museums. The war's monstrous cruelty also fueled movements toward international cooperation. The United Nations was founded in 1945, aiming to prevent future global conflicts, though the Cold War quickly tested its effectiveness.

Unending Searches for Truth

Decades after 1945, historians, family researchers, and even treasure hunters continued to seek answers about the war. Some looked for hidden art or gold, as described in earlier chapters. Others searched declassified archives to uncover lost details of espionage or secret battles. Survivors gave interviews, recorded memoirs, or donated personal letters to museums, gradually revealing stories that were once too painful or too dangerous to share. As new generations inherited wartime letters, medals, and artifacts, they pursued genealogical leads to fill gaps in their family histories.

Occasionally, startling discoveries still happened. A long-lost plane might be found in a remote swamp, the pilot's remains finally given a proper burial. A sealed bunker in Europe could yield crates of documents or personal items. Each find provided fresh insight into how individuals lived, fought, or survived. Meanwhile, in the Pacific, unexploded ordnance and sunken ships served as reminders of battles that once raged across tropical islands. Archaeologists studied these sites to understand the daily realities of soldiers, not just the strategic stories found in official records. The war's physical traces, gradually eroded by time, still carried silent witnesses to events that shaped the modern world.

Lessons and Lingering Shadows

World War II forever changed politics, technology, and society. Nations drew lessons about alliances, deterrence, and the fragile nature of peace. At the same time, the shadow of nuclear weapons and the memory of genocide warned everyone that future wars could be even worse. Some survivors devoted their lives to promoting peace and understanding, speaking out against hate and discrimination. Others nursed resentments or found themselves locked in new struggles. The Cold War that followed soon overshadowed the immediate aftermath, shifting attention to the rivalry between superpowers. But the moral questions posed by World War II lingered, forcing every generation to revisit them.

In the end, the war's unresolved mysteries—be they lost artifacts, missing people, or hidden documents—remained a testament to the vast scale of this global conflict. Historians still debate certain battles' details, and families still discover surprising facts about their ancestors' roles. As the number of firsthand witnesses dwindles, the importance of preserving records, diaries, and oral histories grows. Some mysteries might never be solved, locked forever in memories that did not survive the war. Yet each small revelation helps piece together the puzzle, ensuring that World War II's legacy continues to instruct and caution humanity.

Closing Thoughts

This book has journeyed from the war's early tensions and odd events to its strangest strategies, wildest characters, daring escapes, and final twists. We have seen how people's lives were shaped not just by grand battles but by unforeseen coincidences, acts of bravery, hidden treasures, and medical breakthroughs. The war showed humanity at its worst and best, unleashing cruelty on a massive scale while also sparking incredible compassion and ingenuity. Even now, these stories captivate us precisely because they blend the familiar and the unbelievable, reminding us that the largest conflict in history was more than dates and campaigns—it was a collection of human experiences, both tragic and heroic.

As we conclude with the aftermath and unresolved mysteries, we realize World War II did not simply "end" on a specific date. Instead, it passed its imprint onto every corner of the globe, shaping the policies, economies, and cultural identities of future generations. The pursuit of truth about missing artifacts, unknown fates, or last-minute deals continues to fascinate historians and casual readers alike. By studying these events, perhaps we gain a deeper appreciation for how fragile our world can be, and how essential it is to remember those who endured these difficult years. In a sense, the war remains with us, not as an ongoing tragedy but as a vast tapestry of lessons and questions that will never be fully exhausted. Thank you for reading.

Help Us Share Your Thoughts!

Dear reader,

Thank you for spending your time with this book. We hope it brought you enjoyment and a few new ideas to think about. If there was anything that didn't work for you, or if you have suggestions on how we can improve, please let us know at **kontakt@skriuwer.com**. Your feedback means a lot to us and helps us make our books even better.

If you enjoyed this book, we would be very grateful if you left a review on the site where you purchased it. Your review not only helps other readers find our books, but also encourages us to keep creating more stories and materials that you'll love.

By choosing Skriuwer, you're also supporting **Frisian**—a minority language mainly spoken in the northern Netherlands. Although **Frisian** has a rich history, the number of speakers is shrinking, and it's at risk of dying out. Your purchase helps fund resources to preserve and promote this language, such as educational programs and learning tools. If you'd like to learn more about Frisian or even start learning it yourself, please visit **www.learnfrisian.com**.

Thank you for being part of our community. We look forward to sharing more books with you in the future.

Warm regards,
The Skriuwer Team

9 783819 717666